BOOK OF CHANTS

BOOK OF CHANTS:

CONSISTING MOSTLY OF

SELECTIONS FROM THE SACRED SCRIPTURES, ADAPTED TO APPROPRIATE MUSIC,

AND

ARRANGED FOR CHANTING

LOWELL MASON

GYAN

Published by

Gyan Publishing House
5, Ansari Road
Daryaganj, New Delhi-110002
Phone: 011-47034999, 9811692060
E-mail: books@gyanbooks.com

Distribution Network
gyanbooks.com
India, USA, Canada, UK, Australia

ISBN: 978-93-7014-419-4 (HB)

First Published, 1845

2nd Impression 2025

Printed at: Gyan Press, Delhi.

BOOK OF CHANTS
Author: LOWELL MASON

BOOK OF CHANTS:

CONSISTING MOSTLY OF

SELECTIONS FROM THE SACRED SCRIPTURES,

ADAPTED TO APPROPRIATE MUSIC,

AND

ARRANGED FOR CHANTING.

DESIGNED FOR

CONGREGATIONAL USE IN PUBLIC OR SOCIAL WORSHIP

"Let the PEOPLE praise thee, O God;
Let ALL THE PEOPLE praise thee."

BY LOWELL MASON.

BOSTON:
WILKINS, CARTER, & CO.
16 WATER STREET.
1845.

PREFACE.

It is gratifying to know that chanting has been gradually finding its way into the devotional exercises of Christians of various denominations within a few years past; and still more so, to be assured that wherever it has been judiciously introduced, and appropriately performed, it has met with the warm approbation of those who feel a deep interest in the spirituality of religious worship.

There is something so decidedly devotional in this style of singing, that it cannot fail to call forth the sympathies of the pious heart. A chant when performed by a well trained choir in appropriate style, and with just expression, unites the eloquence of Sacred music and poetry; and surely, no one who is susceptible of religious emotion can listen to the lofty and sublime strains of David, Isaiah, and other inspired writers, when thus sung, and remain unmoved. The fact that in chanting, the very words of the sacred Scriptures may be used, is certainly much in its favor, and of itself sufficient to commend it to those who desire to make "the statutes of the Lord their songs in the house of their pilgrimage."

It is also much in favor of chanting that there is in it less tendency to draw attention to itself, than there is in Metrical Psalmody, especially, when, as is too often the case in the latter, the principal object seems to be to perform a pleasing air or melody; or to make the music or tune the principal thing, regarding the words as only of secondary importance. Nothing is more to be deprecated in Church Music, than the constant tendency to mere musical display or exhibition. But chanting seems almost to preclude the very idea of diplay; it makes music a servant, altogether secondary to the great object of religious worship, and leaves the mind free and open to the full impression of the sacred text. The beautiful simplicity of the chant; its adaptedness to a clear enunciation of the words, to pause and emphasis; its susceptibility of genuine expression; and its total dissimilarity to Secular Music, are all considerations which seem to render it peculiarly appropriate to religious worship. In addition to which it may be mentioned as an important circumstance rendering the general introduction of chanting desirable, that it is an exercise in which it is quite practicable for the whole congregation to engage. If at first thought it may not appear so easy for a large congregation to keep together in a chant, as in the uniform rhythmically constructed choral; and if it be true indeed, that no one can *chant well*, or bring out the *full effect* of chanting, who has not within him the elements of a good reader; still experience has proved that there is no difficulty in making this a congregational exercise, at once pleasing and edifying, which may not be overcome by a moderate degree of attention to it, at least in those congregations where there is a good choir or precentor to lead. Indeed, it is believed that with the same attention to this subject which has usually been given to the singing of psalms and hymns, congregations may chant much better than they can now sing Metrical Psalmody.

Let chanting be introduced into the Sabbath school, (and what style of singing can be better for a Sabbath school than this?) let it make a part of the devotional exercises of every Sabbath, and it will not be long before it may be successfully introduced into the congregation.

It is the design of this work to furnish a book of chants which can be used by the whole congregation in connection with the common hymn book, so that a part of the singing every Sabbath, or whenever the minister shall think it best, may consist of these beautiful, scriptural and highly devotional pieces. The number of selections might have been increased had it been thought advisable to enlarge the size of the book; but as it is, it will be found to contain a large portion of those passages of the Word of God, suitable for the purposes of public worship, with all the variety that can be required.

In selecting and composing the music, it has been the aim of the editor to insert only such chants as are simple and easy of performance. What others can be suitable for the service of the church? The first point has been to have the musical sounds quite within the compass of the voice, so that each part may be sung with but little effort by the class of voices for which it is designed. The next, which is equally important, has been to introduce no progressions either in melody or harmony that are not of the most easy and natural kind. There has been no attempt at difficult chords; indeed, in conformity with the excellent rule of Dr. Crotch, and the example of the veteran in church music, Kocher, very few dissonant chords have been introduced, except the soft one of five-four in the cadence; and in but few instances has any other than a common chord in its natural position been used for the reciting part of the chant. The idea of chanting a long line to a dissonant chord, and thus keeping the ear in constant suspense and expectation of a resolution, is quite absurd. The mind must be at perfect ease to enable one to enter fully into the sentiment; but this cannot be, while it is employed in calculating a dissonance, or waiting in anxious expectation of its resolution. In several instances, the same chant has been set to different selections; and the same successions of chords will often be found in the cadences of different chants. Utility and not novelty has been constantly kept in view in the preparation of this work.

It is hardly necessary to give any particular directions in relation to the application of the words to the music, as the manner of doing this is sufficiently indicated by the bars inserted in the poetry, conforming to those in the music. The necessity for a division or union of notes in the cadences will be easily perceived, by the number of syllables, or by a dash.

In conclusion, it only remains to commend this book to the blessing of Him whose praises it is intended to set forth, and to express the desire that He would give it success just so far as it may be made instrumental in promoting His glory, and the edification of those who worship him in spirit and in truth.

See "Remarks on Chanting" at the end of this volume.

SELECTION 1. [Ps. 8.]

1 O Lord our Lord,
How excellent is thy name in|all the|earth!
2 Who hast set thy|glo..ry a-| bove the | heavens.
3 Out of the mouth of babes and sucklings
Hast thou ordained strength, be-|cause of..thine|enemies;
4 That thou mightest still the | ene..my | and..the a-| venger.

5 When I consider thy heavens, the work of thy fingers;
The moon and the stars, which | thou..hast or-| dained:
6 What is man, that thou art mindful of him?
And the son of | man,..that thou | visi-test | him.

7 For thou hast made him a little lower than the angels,
And hast crowned him with | glory..and | honor.
8 Thou madest him to have dominion over the work of thy hands;
Thou hast put | all things | under..his | feet.

9 All sheep and oxen, yea, and the beasts of the field;
The fowl of the air, and the fish of the sea,
And whatsoever passeth through the | paths..of the | sea.
10 O Lord our Lord,
How excellent is thy | name in | all the | earth.

CHANT No. 2.

SELECTION 2. [Ps. 5.]

1 Give ear to my words, O LORD;
Consider my | medi-| tation.

2 Hearken unto the voice of my cry, my King, and my God;
For unto | thee will | I— | pray.

3 My voice shalt thou hear in the morning, O LORD;
In the morning will I direct my prayer unto thee, and | will look | up.

4 For thou art not a God that hath pleasure in wickedness,
Neither shall | evil | dwell with | thee.

5 The foolish shall not stand in thy sight;
Thou hatest all | workers..of in-| iquity.

6 Thou shalt destroy them that speak falsehood;
The LORD will abhor the | bloody...and de-| ceitful | man.

7 But as for me, I will come into thy house
In the multitude of thy mercy;
And in thy fear will I worship toward thy | holy | temple.

8 Lead me, O LORD, in thy righteousness, because of mine enemies;
Make thy way | straight be-| fore my | face.

9 Let all those that put their trust in thee rejoice:
Let them ever shout for joy, because|thou de-|fendest them.

10 Let them also that love thy | name be | joyful..in | thee.

11 For thou, LORD, wilt bless the righteous;
With favor wilt thou compass him | as..with a | shield.

12 Thou, Lord, wilt bless the righteous;
With favor wilt thou | compass..him | as..with a | shield.

SELECTION 3. [Is. lix. 1, 2.]

1 Behold, the LORD's hand is not shortened, that it cannot save;
Neither his ear heavy, that it | cannot | hear:

2 But your iniquities have separated between you and your God,
And your sins have hid his face from you,
That | he — | will not | hear.

ch. lv. 7.

3 Let the wicked forsake his way.
And the unrighteous | man his | thoughts:

4 And let him return unto the LORD,
And he will have mercy upon him;
And to our GOD, for | he..will a-| bundant-ly | pardon.

Ez. xxxiii. 11.

5 As I live, saith the LORD GOD,
I have no pleasure in the death of the wicked;
But that the wicked turn from his | way and | live:

6 Turn ye, turn ye, from your evil ways;
For why will ye | die, O | house of | Israel.

SELECTION 4. [Is. lv. 1.]

1 Ho, every one that thirsteth, come ye to the waters,
And he that hath no money; come ye, | buy and | eat;

2 Yea, come, buy wine and milk
Without | money..and | with-out | price.

3 Wherefore do ye spend money for that which is not bread,
And your labor for that which | satis-fieth | not?

4 Hearken diligently unto me, and eat ye that which is good,
And let your soul de-| light it-| self in | fatness.

5 Incline your ear, and come unto me:
Hear, and your | soul shall | live:

6 And I will make an everlasting covenant with you,
Even the sure | mercies..the | mercies..of | David.

CHANT No. 3.

SELECTION 5. [Ps. 2.]

1 Why do the heathen rage,
And the people imagine a | vain— | thing?
2 The kings of the earth set themselves,
And the rulers take counsel together, against the LORD,
And a-| gainst..his An-| ointed | saying:

3 'Let us break their bands asunder,
And cast away their | cords — | from us.'
4 He that sitteth in the heavens shall laugh;
The Lord shall | have them | in de-| rision.

5 Then shall he speak unto them in his wrath,
And vex them in his | sore dis-| pleasure.
6 'Yet have I set my King
Upon my | holy | hill of | Zion.'

7 I will declare the decree:
The Lord hath said unto me 'Thou art my Son;
This day have | I be-| gotten thee.
8 Ask of me, and I will give thee
The heathen for thine inheritance,
And the uttermost parts of the | earth for | thy pos-| session

9 Thou shalt break them with a rod of iron;
Thou shalt dash them in pieces | like a..potter's | vessel.'
10 Be wise now, therefore, O ye kings;
Be in-| structed,..ye | judges..of the | earth.

11 Serve the Lord with fear,
And re-| joice with | trembling.
12 Kiss the Son, lest he be angry,
And ye perish from the way,
When his wrath is kindled but a little.
Blessed are all they that put their | trust, their | trust in | him

1 The Lord reigneth, let the earth rejoice;
Let the multitude of isles be | glad there-| of.

2 Clouds and darkness are round about him:
Righteousness and judgment are the habi-| ta-tion | of his |
throne.

3 A fire goeth before him,
And burneth up his enemies | round a-| bout.

4 His lightnings enlightened the world:
The | earth — | saw and | trembled.

5 The hills melted like wax at the presence of the Lord.
At the presence of the Lord of the | whole — | earth.

6 The heavens declare his righteousness,
And all the | people | see his | glory.

7 Confounded be all they that serve graven images,
That boast themselves of idols: worship him,| all ye | gods.

8 Zion heard, and was glad;
And the daughters of Judah rejoiced,
Because of thy | judgments, | O — | Lord.

9 For thou, Lord, art high above all the earth;
Thou art exalted far above | all — | gods.

10 Ye that love the Lord, hate evil:
He preserveth the souls of his saints;
He delivereth them out of the | hand — | of the | wicked.

11 Light is sown for the righteous,
And gladness for the | upright..in | heart.

12 Rejoice in the Lord, ye righteous;
And give thanks at the re-| membrance | of his | holiness.

CHANT No. 4.

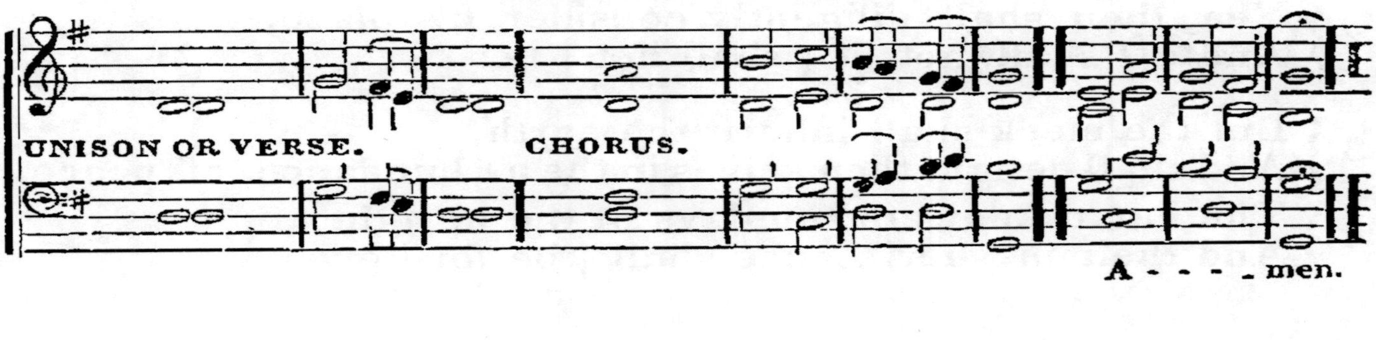

CHANT No. 5.

SELECTION 7. [Ps. 1]

1 Blessed is the man
That walketh not in the counsel of the ungodly,
Nor standeth in the way of sinners,
Nor sitteth in the | seat..of the | scornful;

2 But his delight is in the law of the LORD,
And in his law doth he | medi-tate | day and | night.

3 And he shall be like a tree
Planted by the rivers of water,
That bringeth forth his | fruit..in his | season.

4 His leaf also shall not wither;
And whatso-| ever..he | doeth..shall | prosper.

5 The ungodly are not so;
But are like the chaff which the wind | driveth..a-| way.

6 Therefore the ungodly shall not stand in the judgment,
Nor sinners in the congre-| ga-tion | of the | righteous

7 For the LORD knoweth the way of the righteous,
But the way of the un- | godly..shall | perish.

8 The LORD knoweth the way of the righteous,
But the | way .. of th'un | godly .. shall | perish.

SELECTION 8. [From Ps. 37.]

1 For yet a little while, and the wicked | shall not | be.

2 Yea, thou shalt diligently consider his place,
And it | shall..not, it | shall not | be

3 But the meek shall inherit the earth,
And shall delight themselves in the a-| bundance..of | peace.

4 The LORD knoweth the days of the upright;
And their in-| heri..tance shall | be for-| ever

CHANT No. 6.

SELECTION 9. [Ps. xc. 1–12.]

1 LORD, thou hast been our dwelling place
In | all gene-| rations.
2 Before the mountains were brought forth,
Or ever thou hadst formed the earth and the world,
Even from everlasting, to ever-| lasting, | Thou art | God.

3 Thou turnest man to destruction;
And sayest, Return, ye | chil..dren of | men.
4 For a thousand years in thy sight
Are but as yesterday when it is past,
And | as a | watch..in the | night.

5 Thou carriest them away as with a flood;
They are as a sleep:
In the morning they are like grass which | groweth | up.
6 In the morning it flourisheth, and groweth up;
In the evening it is cut | down, *cut* | *down* and | withereth.

7 For we are consumed by thine anger,
And by thy | wrath..are we | troubled.
8 Thou hast set our iniquities before thee,
Our secret sins in the | light of | thy — | countenance.

9 For all our days are passed away in thy wrath;
We spend our years as a | tale..that is | told.
10 The days of our years are threescore years and ten;
And if by reason of strength they be fourscore years,
Yet is their strength labor and sorrow:
For it is soon cut | off..and we | fly a-| way.

11 Who knoweth the power of thine anger?
Even according to thy fear, | so is..thy | wrath.
12 So teach us to number our days,
That we may ap | ply our | hearts..unto | wisdom.

CHANT No. 7.

SELECTION 10. [Ps. 3.]

1 { Lord, how are they multiplied that trouble me!
{ Many are they that rise | up a-| gainst me.

2 { Many there be which say of my soul,
{ There is no | help for | him in | God.

3 { But thou, O Lord, art a shield for me;
{ My Glory and the Lifter | up of..my | head.

4 { I cried unto the Lord with my voice,
{ And he heard me from his | ho..ly, his | holy | hill.

5 { I laid me down and slept,
{ I awaked; for the | Lord sus-| tained me.

6 { I will not be afraid of ten thousands of people
{ That have set themselves a-| gainst me | round a-| bout.

7 { Arise, O Lord, save me, O my God;
{ For thou hast smitten all mine enemies upon the cheek-bone;
{ Thou hast broken the | teeth..of th'un-| godly.

8 { Salvation belongeth unto the Lord;
{ Thy | blessing..is up-| on thy | people.

SELECTION 11. [Ps. 85.]

1 { Turn us, O God of our salvation,
{ And cause thine anger | toward..us to | cease.

2 { Wilt thou be angry with us forever?
{ Wilt thou draw out thine | anger..to | all..gene-| rations?

3 { Wilt thou not revive us again,
{ That thy people may re-| joice in | thee?

4 { Show us thy mercy, O Lord,
{ And | grant us | thy sal-| vation.

SELECTION 12. [Is. liii. 3–6.]

1 He is despised and rejected of men;
A man of sorrows, and ac-| quainted..with | grief:

2 And we hid as it were our faces from him;
He was despised, and | we es-| teemed..him | not.

3 Surely he hath borne our griefs,
And | carried..our | sorrows:

4 Yet we did esteem him stricken:
| Smitten..of | God,..and af-| flicted.

5 But he was wounded for our transgressions,
He was bruised for | our in-| iquities.

6 The chastisement of our peace was upon him,
And | with his | stripes..we are | healed.

7 All we, like sheep, have gone astray;
We have turned every one to | his own | way.

8 And the LORD hath laid on him, the in-| iqui-ty | of us | all.

SELECTION 13. [Ps. 61.]

1 Hear my cry, O God,
Attend un-| to my | prayer

2 From the end of the earth will I cry unto thee,
When my heart is overwhelmed:
Lead me to the | Rock..that is | higher..than | I

3 For thou hast been a shelter for me,
And a strong | tower..from the | enemy.

4 I will abide in thy tabernacle forever:
I wil: trust in the | covert..of | thy — | wings.

CHANT No. 8.

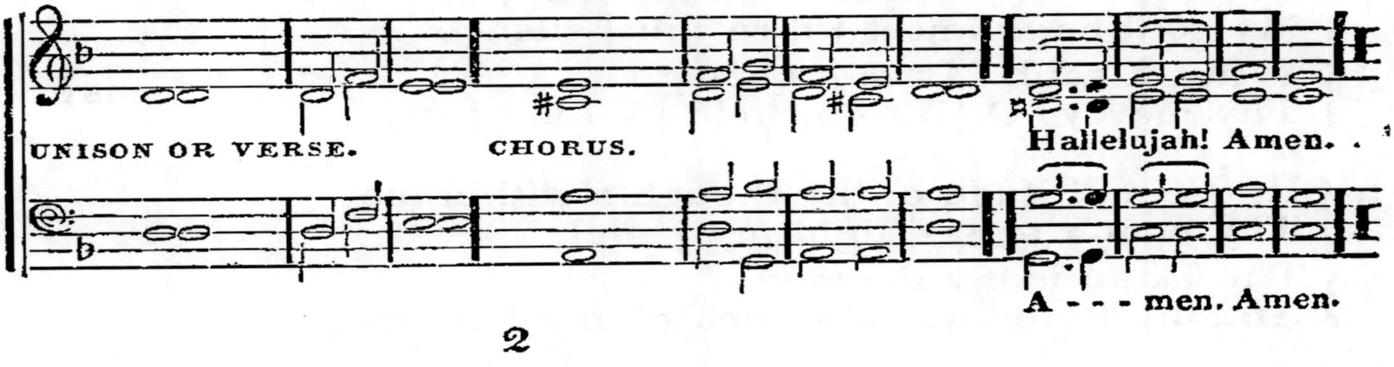

CHANT No. 9.

SELECTION 14.

[Ps. 13.]

1 How long wilt thou forget me, O | Lord? for-| ever?
2 How long wilt thou hide thy | face, thy | face —| from me?

3 { How long shall I take counsel in my soul,
Having sorrow in my | heart — | daily?
4 How long shall mine enemy be ex-| alted | over | me?

5 Consider and hear me, O | Lord my | God;
6 Lighten mine eyes, lest I | sleep the | sleep of | death.

7 Lest mine enemy say, I have pre-| vailed..a-| gainst him;
8 And those that trouble me re-| joice when | I am | moved.

9 { But I have trusted in thy mercy,
My heart shall rejoice in | thy sal-| vation.
10 { I will sing unto the Lord,
Because he hath dealt | bounti..fully | with — | me.

SELECTION 15.

[From Ps. 94.]

1 { Unless the Lord had been my help,
My soul had almost | dwelt in | silence.
2 { When I said, My foot slippeth,
Thy mercy, O | Lord, held | — me | up.

3 { In the multitude of thy thoughts within me
Thy comforts de-| light my | soul.
4 { The Lord is my defence;
And my | God..is the | rock of..my | refuge.

SELECTION 16. [Ps. cxvi. 1–8.]

1 I love the LORD, because he hath heard
My voice, and my | sup-pli-| cations.
2 Because he hath inclined his ear unto me,
Therefore will I call upon | him, as | long..as I | live.

3 The sorrows of death encompassed me,
And the pains of hell got hold upon me:
I found | trouble..and | sorrow.
4 Then called I upon the name of the LORD:
O LORD, I beseech thee, de-| liver..de-| liver..my | soul.

5 Gracious is the LORD, and righteous,
Yea, our | God is | merciful.
6 The LORD preserveth the simple;
I was brought | low, and | he — | helped me.

7 Return unto thy rest, O my soul;
For the LORD hath dealt | bounti..fully | with thee.
8 For thou hast preserved my soul from death,
Mine eyes from | tears..and my | feet from | falling.

SELECTION 17. [Ps.cxvi.12–19.]

1 What shall I render unto the LORD
For all his | bene..fits | toward me?
2 I will take the cup of salvation,
And | call up..on the | name..of the | Lord.

3 I will pay my vows unto the LORD
Now, in the presence of | all his | people.
4 Precious in the sight of the LORD
Is the | death of | his — | saints.

5 O LORD, truly I am thy servant;
I am thy servant, and the son of thy handmaid;
Thou hast | loosed..my | bonds.
6 I will offer to thee the sacrifice of thanksgiving,
And will | call up..on the | name..of the | LORD

7 I will pay my vows unto the LORD
Now, in the presence of | all his | people.
8 In the courts of the LORD's house,
In the midst of thee, O Jerusalem.
| Praise — | ye the | LORD.

CHANT No. 10.

SELECTION 18. [Ps. xcvi.]

1 O sing unto the LORD a new song;
Sing unto the LORD, | all the | earth.

2 Sing unto the LORD, bless his name:
Show forth his sal-| vation..from | day to | day.

3 Declare his glory among the heathen,
His wonders a-| mong all | people.

4 For the LORD is great, and greatly to be praised,
He is to be | feared a-| bove all | gods.

5 For all the gods of the nations are idols;
But the | LORD..made the | heavens.

6 Honor and majesty are before him;
Strength and | beauty..are | in his | sanctuary.

7 Give unto the LORD, O ye kindreds of the people,
Give unto the LORD | glory..and | strength:

8 Give unto the LORD the glory due unto his name;
Bring an offering, and | come in-| to his | courts.

9 O worship the LORD in the beauty of holiness:
Fear before him, | all the | earth.

10 Say among the heathen, that the LORD reigneth:
The world also shall be established that it shall not be moved:
He shall | judge the | people | righteously.

11 Let the heavens rejoice, and let the earth be glad;
Let the sea roar, and the | fulness..there-| of.

12 Let the field be joyful, and all that is therein:
Then shall all the trees of the wood
Re-| joice be-| fore the | LORD;

13 For he cometh,
For he cometh to | judge the | earth.
14 He shall judge the world with righteousness,
And the | people | with his | truth.

CHANT NO. 11.

SELECTION 19. [Ps. xxxiii. 1–12.]

1 Rejoice in the LORD, O ye righteous;
For praise is | comely..for the | upright.
2 Praise the LORD with harp,
Sing unto him with the psaltery, and an | instru-ment | of ten | strings.

3 Sing unto him a new song:
Play skilfully with a | loud — | noise:
4 For the word of the LORD is right,
And all his | works are | done in | truth.

5 He loveth righteousness and judgment,
The earth is full of the | goodness..of the | LORD.
6 By the word of the LORD were the heavens made;
And the host of them by the | breath of | his — | mouth.

7 He gathereth the waters of the sea together as an heap:
He layeth up the | depth in | storehouses.
8 Let all the earth fear the LORD;
Let all the inhabitants of the | world..stand in | awe of | him.

9 For he spake, and it was done;
He commanded, and | it stood | fast.
10 The Lord bringeth the counsel of the heathen to nought;
He maketh the devices of the | people..of | none ef-| fect.

11 The counsel of the LORD standeth forever,
The thoughts of his heart to | all..gene-| rations.
12 Blessed is the nation whose God is the LORD:
And the people whom he hath chosen for his | own in-| heri-| tance.

CHANT No. 12.

SELECTION 20.

[Ps. lxv.1–7.]

1 Praise waiteth for thee, O | God, in | Zion:
2 And unto | thee..shall the | vow..be per-| formed.

3 O thou that hearest prayer,
Unto thee shall | all flesh | come.
4 Iniquities prevail against me:
As for our transgressions,| thou shalt | purge..them a-|way.

5 Blessed is the man whom thou choosest,
And causest to approach unto thee,
That he may | dwell in..thy | courts.
6 We shall be satisfied with the goodness
Of thy house, | even..of thy | holy | temple.

7 By terrible things in righteousness
Wilt thou answer us, O God of | our sal-| vation.
8 Who art the confidence of all the ends of the earth,
And of them that are afar | off up-| on the | sea.

9 Who by his strength setteth fast the mountains;
Being | girded..with | power:
10 Which stilleth the noise of the seas,
The noise of their waves, and the | tumult | of the | people.

11 Praise waiteth for thee, O | God, in | Zion:
12 And unto | thee..shall the | vow..be per-| formed.

SELECTION 21. [Ps. xcv.]

1 O come, let us sing unto the LORD;
Let us make a joyful noise to the Rock of | our sal-| vation.

2 Let us come before his presence with thanksgiving,
And make a joyful | noise..unto | him with | psalms.

3 For the LORD is a great God,
And a great King a-| bove all | gods.

4 In his hand are the deep places of the earth;
The strength of the | hills is | his — | also.

5 The sea is his, and he made it;
And his hands | formed the..dry | land.

6 O come, let us worship and bow down:
Let us kneel be-| fore the | LORD our | Maker.

7 For he is our God; and we are the people of his pasture,
And the | sheep of..his | hand.

8 To-day, if ye will hear his voice,
"Harden not your heart, as in the provocation,
"And as in the day of temptation in the wilderness
"When your fathers tempted me,
| "Proved..me, and | saw my | work.

9 "Forty years long was I grieved with this generation,
"And said, It is a people that do err in their heart,
"And they have not | known my | ways.

10 "Unto whom I sware in my wrath,
"That they should | not..enter | into..my | rest.

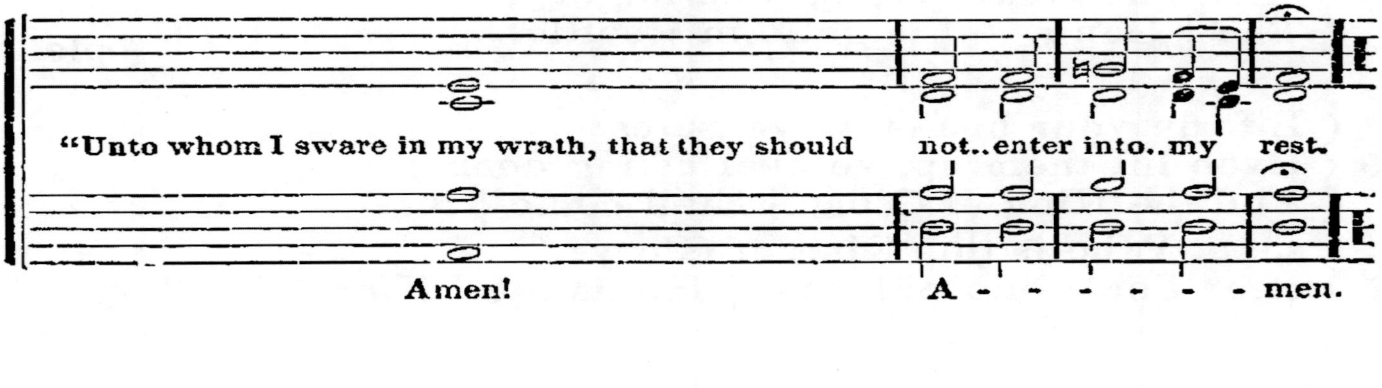

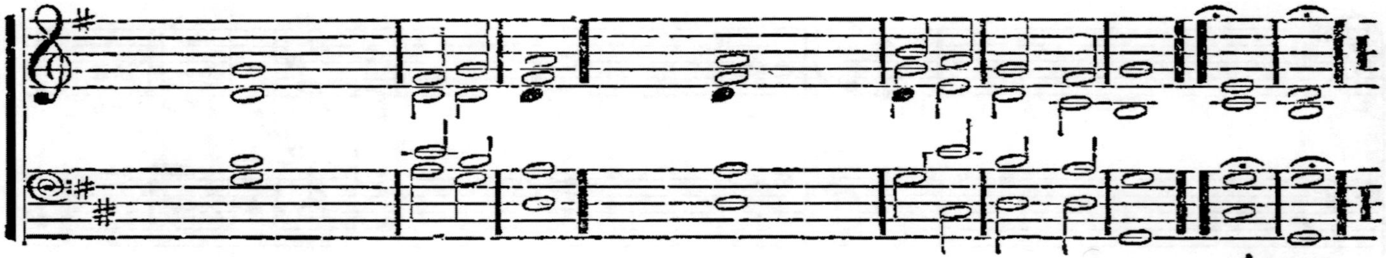

SELECTION 22. [Ps. xxiv.]

CHORUS.

1 { The earth is the LORD's, and the fulness thereof;
The world, and they that | dwell there-| in;

2 { For he hath founded it upon the seas,
And es-| tablish'd..it up-| on the | floods.

SOLO.

3 { Who shall ascend into the hill of the LORD?
And who shall stand in his | holy | place?

CHORUS.

4 { He that hath clean hands, and a pure heart;
Who hath not lifted up his soul unto vanity,
Nor | sworn | de- —| ceitfully.

5 { He shall receive the blessing from the LORD,
And righteousness from the God of | his sal-| vation.

6 { This is the generation of them that seek him,
That | seek thy | face, O | Jacob.

7 { Lift up your heads, O ye gates;
And be ye lift up, ye everlasting doors;
And the King of Glory | shall come | in.

8 { SOLO. Who is this King of Glory?
CHO. The LORD, strong and mighty;
The | LORD — | mighty..in | battle.

9 { Lift up your heads, O ye gates;
Even lift them up, ye everlasting doors;
And the King of Glory | shall come | in.

10 { SOLO. Who is this King of Glory?
CHO. The LORD of hosts, | He..is the | King of | Glory.

1 Praise the Lord, O Jerusalem, praise thy | God, O | Zion.

2 { For he hath strengthened the bars of thy gates;
He hath blessed thy | chil — | dren with- | in thee.

3 { He maketh peace in thy borders,
And filleth thee with the | finest..of | wheat.

4 { He sendeth forth his commandment upon earth:
His | word..runneth | very | swiftly.

5 { He giveth snow like wool:
He scattereth the | hoar-frost..like | ashes.

6 { He casteth forth his ice like morsels:
Who can | stand be- | fore his | cold?

7 { He sendeth out his word, and melteth them:
He causeth his wind to blow, and the | waters | flow.

8 { He showeth his word unto Jacob,
His statutes and his | judgments | unto | Israel.

9 { He hath not dealt so with any nation:
And as for his judgments, they | have not | known them.

10 { Praise ye the Lord,
| Praise — | ye the | Lord.

SELECTION 24. [Rev.iv.8–11.v.10–13.]

1 Holy, holy, holy, | Lord..God Al- | mighty.

2 Which was, and | is, and | is to | come. (sym.)

3 { Thou art worthy, O Lord, to receive glory, and | honor..
and | power;

4 { For thou hast created all things,
And for thy pleasure they | are and | were cre- | ated. (sym.)

5 Worthy is the Lamb | that was | slain,

6 { To receive power, and riches, and wisdom,
And strength, and | honor,..and | glory,..and | blessing. (sym.)

7 Blessing, and honor, and | glory,..and | power,

8 { Be unto him that sitteth upon the throne,
And unto the | Lamb for- | ever..and | ever.

SELECTION 25. [Is. lx. 1–5.]

1 { Arise! shine! for thy light is come,
And the glory of the LORD is | risen..up-| on thee.
2 { For behold, the darkness shall cover the earth,
And | gross — | dark..ness the | people.

3 { But the Lord shall arise upon thee,
And his glory shall be | seen up-| on thee.
4 { And the gentiles shall come to thy light,
And | kings..to the | brightness..of thy | rising.

5 { Lift up thine eyes round about, and see!
All they gather themselves together, they | come to | thee.
6 { Thy sons shall come from far,
And thy | daughters..shall be | nursed..at thy | side.

7 { Then shalt thou see, and flow together,
And thy heart shall fear, and | be en-| larged;
8 { Because the abundance of the sea shall be converted unto [thee.
The forces of the | Gentiles..shall | come to | thee.

SELECTION 26. [Ps. xcix.]

1 { The LORD reigneth; let the people tremble:
He sitteth between the cherubim; let the | earth be | moved.
2 { The LORD is great in Zion,
And he is high above all people;
Let them praise thy great and terrible | name; for | it is | holy.

3 { The king's strength also loveth judgment;
Thou dost establish equity:
Thou executest judgment and | righteous..ness in | Jacob.
4 { Exalt ye the LORD our God,
And worship at his footstool,
For | he — | is — | holy.

5 { Moses and Aaron among his priests,
And Samuel among them that call upon his name:
They called upon the LORD, and | he — | answer'd them.
6 { He spake unto them in the cloudy pillar:
They kept his testimonies,
And the | ordi..nance | that he | gave them.

7 { Thou didst answer them, O LORD our God;
Thou wast a God that forgavest them,
Though thou tookest vengeance of | their in-| ventions.
8 { Exalt the LORD our God, and worship at his holy hill:
For the | Lord our | God is | holy.

SELECTION 27. [Ps. cxv. 9–18.]

1 { O Israel, trust thou in the LORD:
He is their | help..and their | shield.
2 { O house of Aaron, trust in the LORD,
| He..is their | help..and their | shield.

3 { Ye that fear the Lord, trust in the Lord:
He is their | help..and their | shield.
4 { The Lord hath been mindful of us: he will bless us:
He will bless the house of Israel,
| He will..bless the | house of | Aaron.

5 He will bless them that fear the Lord, both | small and | great.
6 { The LORD shall increase you more and more,
| You and | your — | children.

7 Ye are blessed of the Lord, who made | heaven and | earth.
8 { The heaven, even the heavens are the LORD's,
But the earth hath he | given..to the | children..of | men.

9 { The dead praise not the LORD,
Neither any that go | down..into | silence.
10 { But we will bless the LORD,
From this time forth and forevermore. | Praise — | ye the | Lord.

SELECTION 28. [Ps. cxviii. 1–6, 8, 9, & 29.]

1 { O give thanks unto the LORD, for he is good;
Because his mercy en-| dureth..for-| ever.
2 Let Israel now say, that his | mercy..en-| dureth..for-| ever.

3 { Let the house of Aaron now say,
That his mercy en-| dureth..for | ever.
4 { Let them now that fear the Lord, say
That his | mercy..en-| dureth..for-| ever.

5 { I called upon the LORD in distress;
The LORD answered me, and set me in a | large — | place.
6 { The Lord is on my side; I will not fear:
What can | man do | unto | me?

7 { It is better to trust in the Lord,
Than to put | confi..dence in | man.
8 { It is better to trust in the Lord,
Than to put | con-fi-| dence in | princes.

9 { O give thanks unto the Lord, for he is good;
For his mercy en-| du-reth for-| ever.
10 { O give thanks unto the Lord, for he is good;
For his | mercy..en-| dureth..for-| ever.

SELECTION 29. [Ps. lxxxiv.]

1 How amiable are thy tabernacles, O | Lord of | hosts'

2 My soul longeth, yea, even fainteth
For the courts of the Lord;
My heart and my flesh crieth | out..for the | living | God

3 Yea, the sparrow hath found an house,
And the swallow a nest for herself,
Where she may lay her young,
Even thine altars, O Lord of hosts, my | King and..my | God.

4 Blessed are they that dwell in thy house:
They | will be | still..praising | thee. (sym.)

5 Blessed is the man whose strength is in thee:
In whose heart are the | ways of | them.

6 Who, passing through the valley of Baca, make it a well;
The | rain..also | filleth..the | pools.

7 They go from strength to strength;
Every one of them in Zion appeareth be-| fore — | God.

8 O Lord God of hosts, hear my prayer:
Give | ear, O | God of | Jacob. (sym)

9 Behold, O God, our shield,
And look upon the face of | thine an-| ointed.

10 For a day in thy courts is better than a thousand.
I had rather be a door-keeper in the house of my God,
Than to | dwell..in the | tents of | wickedness.

11 For the Lord God is a sun and shield:
The Lord will give grace and glory:
No good thing will he withhold from them that | walk up-|
rightly.

12 O Lord of hosts, blessed is the | man that | trusteth..in | thee.

SELECTION 30. [Ps. lxvi. 1–4. 13–14. 16–20.]

1 Make a joyful noise unto God, | all ye | lands:

2 Sing forth the honor of his name:
| Make his | praise — | glorious.

3 Say unto God, How terrible art thou in thy works!
Through the greatness of thy power
Shall thine enemies submit them-| selves..unto | thee.

4 All the earth shall worship thee,
And shall sing unto thee; they shall | sing to | thy— | name.

5 I will go into thy house, with | burnt — | offerings;

6 I will pay thee my vows, which my lips have uttered,
And my mouth hath | spoken..when | I..was in | trouble.

7 Come and hear, all ye that fear God,
And I will declare what he hath | done for..my | soul.
8 I cried unto him with my mouth,
And | he..was ex | tolled..with my | tongue.

9 If I regard iniquity in my heart,
The LORD | will not | hear me.
10 But verily God hath heard me;
He hath attended to the | voice of | my — | prayer.

11 Blessed be God, who hath not turned a-| way my | prayer.
12 Who hath not turned away my prayer,
| Nor his | mercy | from me.

SELECTION 31. [Ps. xxx.]

1 I will extol thee, O LORD; for thou hast lifted me up,
And hast not made my foes to re | joice — | over me.
2 O LORD my God, I cried unto thee, and | thou hast | healed | me.

3 O LORD, thou hast brought up my soul from the grave:
Thou hast kept me alive, that I should not go | down..
to the | pit.
4 Sing unto the LORD, O ye saints of his,
And give thanks at the re-| membrance | of his | holiness.

5 For his anger endureth but a moment; in his | favor..is | life:
6 Weeping may endure for a night,
But | joy..cometh | in the | morning.

7 And in my prosperity I said, I shall | never..be | moved.
8 LORD, by thy favor thou hast made my mountain to stand
strong:
Thou didst hide thy | face and | I was | troubled.

9 I cried to thee, O LORD;
And unto the Lord I made | suppli-| cation.
10 What profit is there in my blood, when I go down to the pit?
Shall the dust praise thee? | shall it..de-| clare thy | truth?

11 Hear, O LORD, and have mercy upon me:
LORD, be | thou my | helper.
12 Thou hast turned for me my mourning into dancing:
Thou hast put off my sackcloth, & | girded | me with | gladness.

13 To the end that my glory may sing praise to thee,
And | not be | silent.
14 O LORD my God, I will give thanks unto thee forever;
I will give | thanks..unto | thee for-| ever.

SELECTION 32. [Ps. cxlv. 1–7.]

1 { I will extol thee, my God, O King;
And I will bless thy name for-| ever..and | ever.

2 { Every day will I bless thee,
And I will praise thy | name for-| ever..and | ever.

3 { Great is the Lord, and greatly to be praised;
And his greatness | is un-| searchable.

4 { One generation shall praise thy works to another,
And shall de-| clare thy | mighty | acts.

5 { I will speak of the glorious honor of thy majesty,
And of thy | wondrous | works.

6 { And men shall speak of the might of thy terrible acts,
And | I..will de-| clare thy | greatness.

7 { They shall abundantly utter the memory of thy great goodness,
And shall | sing of..thy | righteousness.

8 { They shall abundantly utter the memory of thy great goodness,
And shall | sing of | thy — | righteousness.

SELECTION 33. [Ps. cxlv. 8–13.]

1 { The Lord is gracious, and full of compassion:
Slow to anger, and of | great— | mercy.

2 { The Lord is good to all;
And his tender mercies are | over | all his | works.

3 { All thy works shall praise thee, O Lord,
And thy | saints shall | bless thee.

4 { They shall speak of the glory of thy kingdom,
And | talk of | thy — | power.

5 { To make known to the sons of men his mighty acts,
And the glorious majesty of | his — | kingdom.

6 { Thy kingdom is an everlasting kingdom,
And thy dominion en-| dureth..throughout | all..gene-| rations.

SELECTION 34. [Ps.cxlv.14–21]

1 The LORD upholdeth all that fall,
And raiseth up all those that | are..bowed | down.
2 The eyes of all wait upon thee,
And thou givest them their | meat in | due — | season.

3 Thou openest thine hand,
And satisfiest the desire of every | living | creature.
4 The LORD is righteous in all his ways,
And | holy..in | all his | works.

5 The LORD is nigh unto all them that call upon him.
To all that call upon | him in | truth.
6 He will fulfil the desire of them that fear him;
He also will hear their | cry, and | will — | save them.

7 The LORD preserveth all them that love him:
But all the wicked will | he de-| stroy.
8 My mouth shall speak the praise of the LORD:
And let all flesh bless his holy | name for-| ever..and | ever.

CHANT No. 15.

SELECTION 35. [Ps. cl.]

1 PRAISE YE THE LORD. Praise God in his sanctuary.
Praise him in the firmament | of his | power.
2 Praise him for his mighty acts:
Praise him according to his | excel-lent his | excel-lent |
greatness.

3 Praise him with the sound of the trumpet;
Praise him with the | psaltery..and | harp.
4 Praise him with the timbrel and dance;
Praise him with | stringed..instru-| ments and | organs.

5 Praise him upon the loud cymbals:
Praise him upon the | high-sounding | cymbals.
6 Let everything that hath breath praise the LORD.
| Praise ye, | Praise..ye the | LORD.

SELECTION 36. [From Rev]

Hallelujah!
1 For the Lord God om-| nipo-tent | reigneth!

2 The kingdoms of this world are become
The kingdoms of our Lord and of his Christ;
And he shall | reign for-| ever..and | ever.

Hallelujah!
3 We give thee thanks, O Lord God Almighty,
Which art, and wast, and | art to | come.

4 King of | kings, and | Lord of | lords.

Hallelujah!
5 Salvation to our God which sitteth upon the throne,
And | unto..the | Lamb.

6 A — | men! Halle-| lujah..A-| men.

Hallelujah!
7 Blessing, and glory, and wisdom,
And thanksgiving, and honor, and | power, and | might,

8 Be unto our | God for-| ever..and | ever.

Hallelujah!
1 Great and marvellous are thy works,| Lord..God Al-| mighty!
2 Just and true are thy | ways, thou | King of | saints.

Hallelujah!
3 Who shall not fear thee, O Lord, and glorify thy name! For thou | only..art | Holy.
4 For all nations shall come and worship before thee; For thy | judg-ments | are made | manifest.

Hallelujah!
5 Salvation, and glory, and honor, and power, unto the | Lord our | God;
6 For true and | righteous | are his | judgments.

Hallelujah!
7 Praise our God, all | ye his | servants,
8 And ye that | fear him..both | small and | great.

Amen! Hallelujah! Hallelujah!

SELECTION 38. [Rev. xxi. 3–4.]

Hallelujah!
1 Behold, the tabernacle of God | is with | men,
2 And he will dwell with them, and | they shall | be his | people.

3 And God himself shall be with them, and | be their | God.
4 And God shall wipe away all | tears from | their — | eyes.

5 And there shall be no more death, Neither | sorrow..nor | crying.
6 Neither shall there be any more pain; For the former | things are | passed..a-| way.

Hallelujah!
7 Behold the tabernacle of God | is with | men,
8 And he will dwell with them, and | they shall | be his | people.

Amen! Hallelujah! Hallelujah!

CHANT No. 17

SELECTION 39. [Ps. xvi.]

1 Preserve me, O | God,
For in thee do I put my | trust.

2 O my soul, thou hast said unto the Lord,
Thou art | my Lord:
My goodness ex-| tendeth | not to | thee.

3 But to the saints that are in the | earth,
And to the excellent, in whom is all my de-| light.

4 Their sorrows shall be multiplied
That hasten after another | god:
Their drink-offerings of blood will I not offer,
Nor take up their | names in-| to my lips.

5 The Lord is the portion of my inheritance, and of my | cup:
Thou maintainest my | lot.

6 The lines are fallen unto me in pleasant | places:
Yea, I | have a | goodly | heritage.

7 I will bless the Lord, who hath given me | counsel;
My reins also instruct me in the | night-season.

8 I have set the Lord always be-| fore me;
Because he is at my right | hand..I shall | not be | moved.

9 Therefore my heart is glad, and my glory re-| joiceth;
My flesh also shall rest in | hope.

10 For thou wilt not leave my soul in | hell;
Neither wilt thou suffer thine Holy|One to|see cor-|ruption.

11 Thou wilt show me the path of | life.—
Thou wilt show me the path of | life.

12 In thy presence is fullness of | joy;
At thy right hand there are | pleasures..for-| ever-| more.

CHANT No. 18.

SELECTION 40. [Ps. xv.]

1 LORD, who shall abide in thy tabernacle?
Who shall dwell in thy | holy | hill?

2 He that walketh uprightly, and worketh righteousness,
And speaketh the | truth in | his — | heart.

3 He that backbiteth not with his tongue,
Nor doeth evil to his neighbor,
Nor taketh up a reproach a-| gainst his neighbor,

4 In whose eyes a vile person is contemned;
But he honoreth | them that | fear the | LORD.

5 He that sweareth to his own hurt, and changeth not:
He that putteth not out his money to usury,
Nor taketh reward a-| gainst the | innocent.

6 He that doeth these things shall | never..shall | never..be |
moved.

SELECTION 41. [From Ps. xxxvii.]

1 The steps of a good man are ordered by the LORD;
And he de-| lighteth..in his | way.

2 Though he fall, he shall not be utterly cast down;
For the LORD up-| holdeth..him | with his | hand.

3 I have been young, and | now am | old;

4 Yet I have not seen the righteous forsaken,
| Nor his | seed..begging | bread.

5 For the LORD loveth judgment,
And forsaketh | not his | saints:

6 The righteous shall inherit the land,
And | dwell there-| in for-| ever.

CHANT No. 19.

SELECTION 42. [Ps. xx]

1 { The Lord hear thee in the day of trouble;
{ The name of the God of | Jacob..de-| fend thee.

2 { Send thee help from the sanctuary.
{ And | strengthen..thee | out of | Zion.

3 { Remember all thy offerings,
{ And accept thy | burnt — | sacrifice.

4 { Grant thee according to thine own heart,
{ And ful-| fil all | thy — | counsel.

5 { We will rejoice in thy salvation,
{ And in the name of our God we will set | up our | banners.

6 { The Lord fulfil all thy petitions, ful-| fil all | thy pe-|
{ tions.

7 Now know I that the Lord saveth | his an-| ointed.

8 { He will hear him from his holy heaven
{ With the saving | strength of | his right | hand.

9 { Some trust in chariots, and some in horses;
{ But we will remember the name of the | Lord our | God

10 { They are brought down and fallen;
{ But we are | risen..and | stand — | upright.

11 { Save, Lord!
{ Let the king hear us | when we | call.

12 { Save, Lord!
{ Let the king | hear us | when we | call.

CHANT No. 20.

SELECTION 43.

[Ps. xxvi.]

1 Judge me, O LORD;
For I have walked in mine integrity:
I have trusted also in the LORD;
Therefore I | shall not | slide.

2 Examine me, O LORD, and prove me;
| Try my | reins..and my | heart.

3 For thy loving-kindness is before mine eyes:
And I have | walked..in thy | truth.

4 I have not sat with vain persons,
Neither will I go | in — | with dis-| semblers.

5 I have hated the congregation of evil-doers;
And will not | sit..with the | wicked.

6 I will wash my hands in innocency:
So will I compass thine | altar..thine | altar..O | LORD.

7 That I may publish with the voice of thanksgiving,
And tell of all thy | wondrous | works.

8 LORD, I have loved the habitation of thy house,
And the place where thine | honor..thine | honor | dwelleth.

9 Gather not my soul with sinners,
Nor my life with | bloody | men.

10 In whose hands is mischief,
And their right hand is | full, is | full of | bribes.

11 But as for me, I will walk in mine integrity;
Redeem me, and be | merciful..unto | me.

12 My foot standeth in an even place:
In the congregation will I | bless..will I | bless the | LORD.

CHANT No. 21.

SELECTION 44. [Ps. xxxiii.13–22.]

1 The LORD looketh from heaven;
He beholdeth all the | sons of | men.

2 From the place of his habitation he looketh
Upon all the in-| habi-tants | of the | earth.

3 He fashioneth their hearts alike;
He considereth | all their | works.

4 There is no king saved by the multitude of an host:
A mighty man is not de-| livered..by | much — | strength.

5 An horse is a vain thing for safety;
Neither shall he deliver any by | his great | strength.

6 Behold, the eye of the LORD is upon them that fear him.
Upon them that | hope in | his — | mercy;

7 To deliver their soul from death,
And to keep them a-| live in | famine,

8 Our soul waiteth for the LORD;
He is our | help and | our — | shield.

9 For our heart shall rejoice in him;
Because we have trusted in his | holy | name.

10 Let thy mercy, O LORD, be upon us,
According as we | hope..as we | hope in | thee.

CHANT NO. 22.

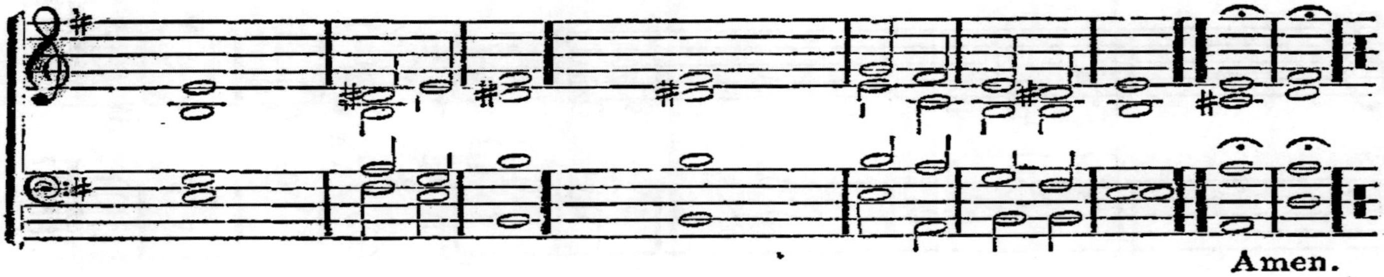

SELECTION 45. [Ps. xxxix. 4–13.]

1 Lord, make to know mine end,
And the measure of my days, | what it | is.
2 That I may know how | frail, how | frail I | am.

3 Behold, thou hast made my days as an handbreadth,
And mine age is as nothing be-| fore — | thee.
4 Verily every man at his best estate,
Is | al-to-| ge-ther | vanity.

5 Surely every man walketh in a vain show;
Surely they are dis-| quie-ted in | vain.
6 He heapeth up riches, and | knoweth..not | who shall |
gather them.

7 And now, Lord, what wait I for?
My | hope..is in | thee.
8 Deliver me from all my transgressions;
Make me | not..the re-| proach..of the | foolish.

9 I was dumb, I opened not my mouth;
Be-| cause thou | didst it.
10 Remove thy stroke away from me:
I am con-| sumed..by the | blow of..thine | hand.

11 When thou with rebukes dost correct man for iniquity,
Thou makest his beauty to consume a-| way..like a |
moth.
12 Surely every man is vanity; | every | man is | vanity.

13 Hear my prayer, O Lord,
And give ear un-| to my | cry;
14 Hold not thy peace, hold | not thy | peace..at my | tears.

15 For I am a stranger with thee,
And a sojourner, as all my | fathers | were.
16 O spare me, that I may recover strength,
Before I go | hence, and | be no | more.

CHANT No. 23.

SELECTION 46.

[Is. xl. 9–11.]

1 O Zion, that bringest good tidings,
Get thee up into the high mountain,
O Jerusalem, that bringest good tidings,
Lift up thy | voice with | strength.

2 Lift it up, be not afraid;
Say unto the cities of | Judah..Be-| hold your | God!

3 Behold, the LORD GOD will come with strong hand,
And his arm shall | rule — | for him:

4 Behold his reward is with him,
And his | work, his | work be-| fore him.

5 He shall feed his flock like a shepherd;
He shall gather the lambs with his arm,
And carry them | in his | bosom.

6 And shall gently lead | those that | are with | young.(SYM.)

7 They that wait upon the LORD shall re-| new their | strength.

8 They shall mount up with wings as eagles;
They shall run and not be weary,
And they shall | walk, shall | walk and..not | faint.

CHANT NO. 24.

SELECTION 47. [Ps. cxxii.]

1 I was glad when they said unto me,
Let us go into the | house..of the | Lord.

2 Our feet shall stand within thy gates, O Jerusalem,
Jerusalem is builded as a city that | is com-|pact to-|gether.

3 Whither the tribes go up; the tribes of the Lord,
Unto the testimony of Israel,
To give thanks unto the | name..of the | Lord.

4 For there are set thrones of judgment,
The | thrones..of the | house of | David.

5 Pray for the peace of Jerusalem,
They shall | prosper..that | love thee.

6 Peace be within thy walls;
And pros-| peri..ty with-| in thy | palaces.

7 For my brethren and companions' sakes,
I will now say, | Peace..be with-| in thee.

8 Because of the house of the Lord our God,
I will | seek, will | seek thy | good.

CHANT No. 26.

SELECTION 48. [Ps. xxvii.]

1 The LORD is my light and my salvation,
| Whom..shall I | fear?

2 The LORD is the strength of my life,
Of | whom..shall I | be a-| fraid? (SYM.)

3 One thing have I desired of the LORD,
| That..will I | seek after;

4 That I may dwell in the house of the LORD
All the days of my life,
To behold the beauty of the LORD,
And to in-| quire..to in-| quire in..his | temple.

5 For in the time of trouble he shall hide me in | his pa-|
vilion;

6 In the secret of his tabernacle shall he hide me;
He shall | set..me up-| on a | rock.

7 And now shall mine head be lifted up
Above mine enemies, | round a-| bout me.

8 Therefore will I offer in his tabernacle sacrifices of joy;
I will sing, yea, I will sing | praises..un-| to the | LORD.

9 Hear, O LORD, when I cry with my voice:
Have mercy also upon me, and | answer | me.

10 When thou saidst, Seek ye my face;
My heart said unto thee, Thy | face, LORD | will I | seek.

11 Hide not thy face far from me;
Put not thy servant a-| way in | anger.

12 Thou hast been my help; leave me not,
Neither forsake me, O | God of | my sal-| vation.

13 When my father and my mother forsake me,
Then the LORD will | take me | up.

14 Teach me thy way, O LORD,
And lead me in a plain path,
Be-| cause of | mine — | enemies.

15 Deliver me not over unto the | will of..mine | enemies;
16 For false witnesses are risen up against me,
And | such as | breathe out | cruelty.

17 I had fainted, unless I had believed to see the goodness
Of the LORD, in the | land..of the | living.
18 Wait on the LORD; be of good courage,
And he shall strengthen thine heart:
| Wait, I | say,..on the | LORD.

CHANT NO. 27.

SELECTION 49. [Micah vii. 18.]

1 Who is like unto thee, that pardoneth iniquity?
And passeth by the transgression
Of the remnant | of his | heritage?
2 He retaineth not his anger forever,
Be-| cause..he de-| lighteth..in | mercy.

3 He will turn again, he will have compassion upon us;
He will sub-| due..our in-| iquities:
4 And thou will cast all their sins into the | depths, the |
depths..of the | sea.

5 Thou wilt perform the truth to Jacob,
And the | mercy..to | Abraham,
6 Which thou hast sworn unto our fathers,
From the | days, the | days of | old.

CHANT No. 28.

SELECTION 50. [Ps. xiv.]

1 { The fool hath said in his heart,
There is | no — | God.

2 { They are corrupt; they have done abominable works;
There is | none that | doeth | good.

3 { The LORD looked down from heaven
Upon the children of men,
To see if there were any that did understand,
And | seek — | God.

4 { They are all gone aside, they are altogether become filthy.
There is none that doeth | good, no, | — not | one.

5 { Have all the workers of iniquity no knowledge?
Who eat up my people as they eat bread,
And call not up-| on the | LORD.

6 { There were they in great fear;
For God is in the gene-| ra-tion | of the | righteous.

7 { Ye have shunned the counsel of the poor;
Because the | LORD..is his | refuge.

8 { Oh that the salvation of Israel were come out of Zion!
When the LORD bringeth back the captivity of his people.
Jacob shall re-| joice, and | Israel..shall be | glad.

CHANT No. 29.

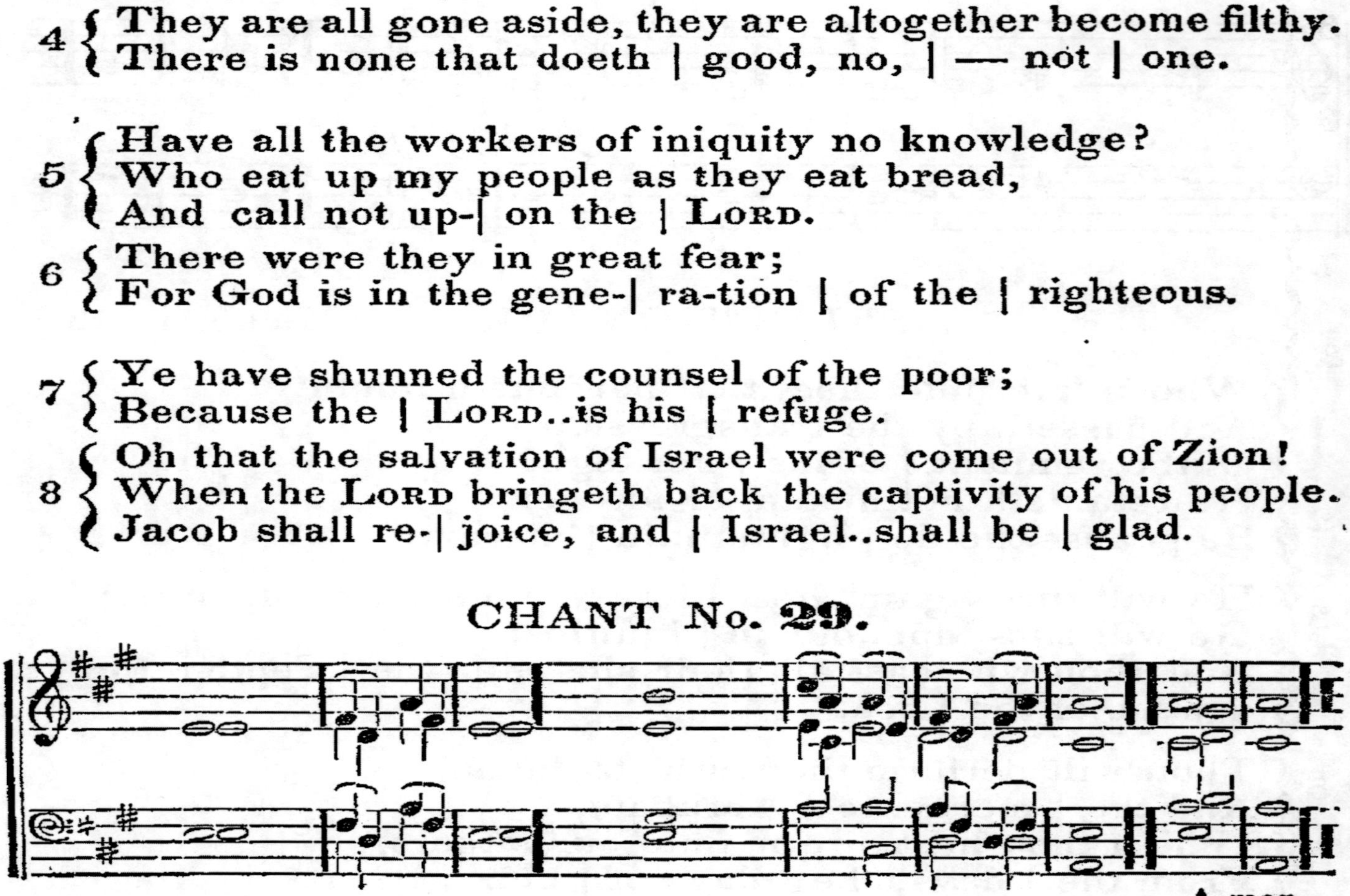

SELECTION 51. [Ps. cxxx.]

1 Out of the depths have I cried unto | thee, O | LORD.

2 LORD, hear my voice;
Let thine ears be attentive to the | voice of..my | suppli-|
cations.

3 If thou, LORD, shouldst mark iniquities,
O LORD, | who shall | stand.

4 But there is forgiveness with thee,
That | thou — | mayest..be | feared.

5 I wait for the LORD, my soul doth wait,
And in his | word..do I | hope.

6 My soul waiteth for the LORD
More than they that watch for the morning,
I say, | more than..they that | watch..for the | morning.

7 Let Israel hope in the LORD:
For with the LORD there is mercy,
And with him is | plenteous..re-| demption.

8 And he shall redeem Israel
From | all — | his in-| iquities.

SELECTION 52. [Ps. lxxiii. 25.]

1 Whom have I in heaven but thee?
And there is none upon earth that I de-| sire be-| side thee.

2 My flesh and my heart faileth;
But God is the strength of my heart, and my | por — |
tion for-| ever.

3 For lo, they that are far from | thee shall | perish.

4 But it is good for me to draw near to God;
I have put my trust in the LORD God,
That I may de-| clare all | thy — | works.

CHANT NO. 31.

SELECTION 53. [Luke i. 46–65.]

1 My soul doth magnify the Lord,
And my spirit hath rejoiced in | God my | Savior.

2 For he hath regarded the low estate of his handmaiden:
For behold, from henceforth all gene-| rations..shall | call me | blessed.

3 For he that is mighty hath done to me great things,
And | holy..is his | name.

4 And his mercy is on them that fear him,
From gene-| ration..to | gene-| ration.

5 He hath showed strength with his arm,
He hath scattered the proud in the imagi-| nation..of their | hearts.

6 He hath put down the mighty from their seats,
And exalted | them of | low de-| gree.

7 He hath filled the hungry with good things,
And hath sent the rich | empty..a-| way.

8 He hath sustained his servant Israel
In remembrance of his mercy.
As he spake to our fathers, to Abraham,
And | to his | seed for-| ever.

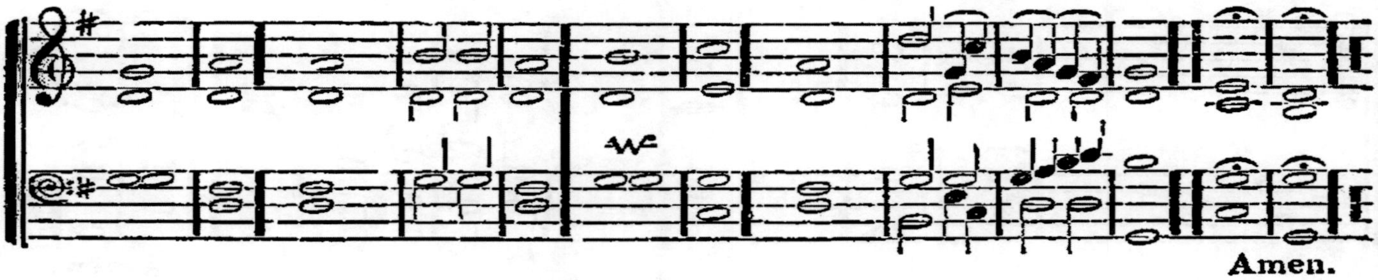

(For the 3d and 5th verses.)

SELECTION 54. [Ps. lxvi.]

1 { God be merciful unto us, and | bless us;
{ And cause his face to | shine up-| on us.

2 { That thy way may be known upon | earth,
{ Thy saving | health a-| mong all | nations.

3 { Let all the people praise thee, O | God;
{ Let | all the..people | praise thee.

4 { O let the nations be glad, and sing for | joy;
{ For thou shalt judge the people righteously,
{ And gòvern the | na..tions up-| on the | earth

5 { Let the people praise thee, O | God;
{ Let | all the..people | praise thee.

6 { Then shall the earth yield her | increase:
{ And | God,..even our | own..God will | bless us.

7 { God shall | bless us;
{ And all the ends of the | earth shall | fear him

8 { God shall | bless us;
{ And all the | ends..of the | earth shall | fear him.

CHANT No. 33.

SELECTION 55. [Is. lv. 6–9.]

1 { Seek ye the Lord while he may be found,
Call ye upon him | while..he is | near.

2 { Let the wicked forsake his way,
And the unrighteous man his thoughts;
And let him return to the Lord, and he will have mercy upon him;
And to our God; for | he..will a-| bundant-ly | pardon.

3 { For *my* thoughts are not *your* thoughts,
Neither are *your* ways *my* ways, | saith the | Lord.

4 { For as the heavens are higher than the earth,
So are my ways higher than your ways,
And | my..thoughts than | your — | thoughts.

CHANT No. 34.

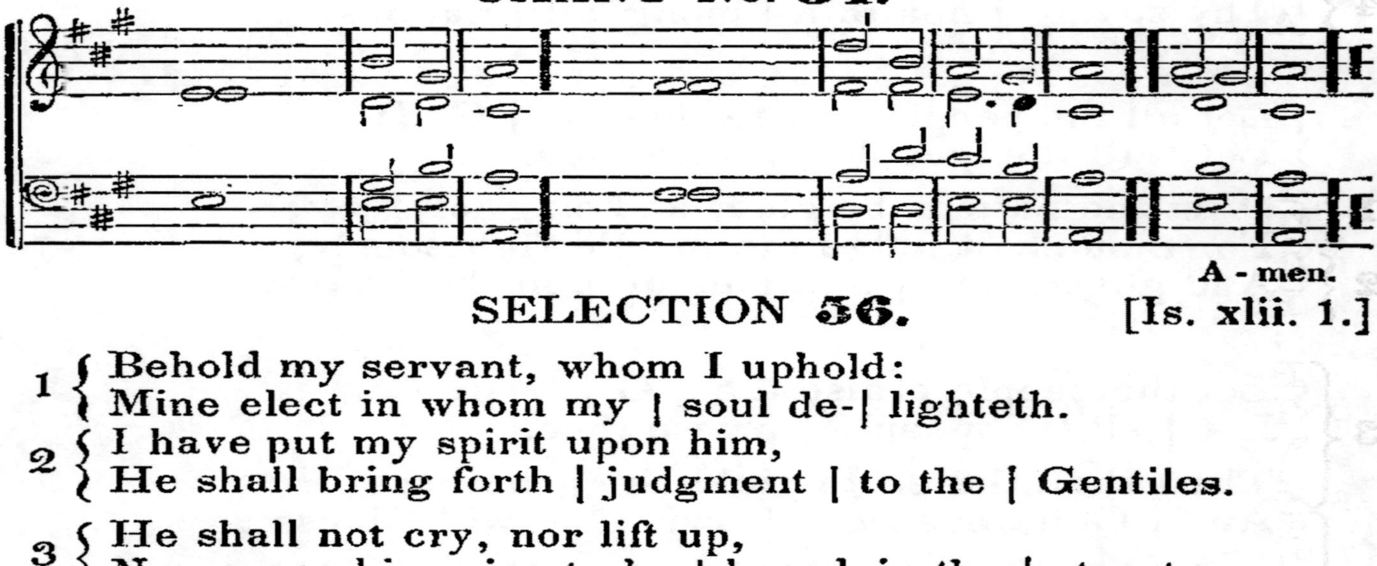

SELECTION 56. [Is. xlii. 1.]

1 { Behold my servant, whom I uphold:
Mine elect in whom my | soul de-| lighteth.

2 { I have put my spirit upon him,
He shall bring forth | judgment | to the | Gentiles.

3 { He shall not cry, nor lift up,
Nor cause his voice to be | heard..in the | street.

4 { A bruised reed shall he not break,
And the smoking flax shall he not quench:
He shall bring forth | judgment | unto | truth.

5 { He shall not fail nor be discouraged,
Till he have set judgment | in the | earth.

6 And the isles shall wait, shall | wait for | his — | law.

SELECTION 57. [Is. li. 9–11.]

1 Awake, awake, put on strength, O arm of the Lord;
Awake, as in the ancient days, in the gene-| rations..of | old.

2 Art thou not it that hath cut Rahab, and wounded the [dragon?
Art thou not it which hath dried the sea,
The waters of the great deep;
That hath made the depths of the sea a way for the | ransom'd to | pass — | over.

3 Therefore the redeemed of the LORD shall return,
And come with singing unto Zion;
And everlasting joy shall be up-| on their | head:

4 They shall obtain gladness and joy;
And sorrow and | mourning..shall | flee a-| way.

SELECTION 58. [Jer. xxxiii. 11,14–16.]

1 The voice of joy, and the voice of gladness;
The voice of the bridegroom, and the | voice..of the| bride.

2 The voice of them that shall say, Praise the LORD of hosts:
For the LORD is good; for his | mercy..en-| dureth..for-| ever.

3 Behold, the days come, saith the LORD,
That I will perform that good thing
Which I have promised unto the house of Israel,
And to the | house of | Judah.

4 In those days, will I cause the Branch of righteousness
To grow up unto David;
And he shall execute judgment and | righteous-ness | in the | land.

5 In those days shall Judah be saved,
And Jerusalem shall | dwell in | safety.

6 And this is the name wherewith he shall be called,
The | LORD, the | LORD our | righteousness.

SELECTION 59. [Ps. li. 1–4. 10–13.]

1 Have mercy upon me, O God,
According to thy | loving-| kindness;
2 According to the multitude of thy tender mercies,
| Blot out | my trans-| gressions.

3 Wash me thoroughly from my iniquity,
And cleanse me | from my | sin.
4 For I acknowledge my transgressions;
And my | sin is | ever..be-| fore me.

5 Against thee, thee only have I sinned,
And done this evil | in thy | sight.
6 That thou mayest be justified when thou speakest,
And be | clear when | thou — | judgest.

7 Create in me a clean heart, O God;
And renew a right | spirit..with | in me.
8 Cast me not away from thy presence;
And take not thy | Ho ly | Spir-it | from me.

9 Restore unto me the joy of thy salvation,
And uphold me with | thy free | Spirit:
10 Then will I teach transgressors thy ways;
And sinners shall be con-| verted | unto | thee.

SELECTION 60. [Ps. lxxx.

1 Give ear, O Shepherd of Israel,
Thou that leadest | Joseph..like a | flock;
2 Thou that dwellest between the | cherubim | shine—| forth.

3 Before Ephraim, and Benjamin, and Manasseh,
Stir up thy strength, and | come and | save us.
4 Turn us again, O God,
And cause thy face to | shine, and | we..shall be | saved.

5 O Lord God of hosts,
How long wilt thou be angry against the | prayer..of thy | people?
6 Thou feedest them with the bread of tears;
And givest them tears to | drink in | great — | measure.

7 Thou makest us a strife to our neighbors;
And our enemies laugh a-| mong them-| selves.
8 Turn us again, O God of hosts,
And cause thy face to | shine; and | we..shall be | saved.

---

9 Thou hast brought a vine out of Egypt;
Thou hast cast out the | heathen,..and | planted it.
10 Thou preparedst room before it,
And didst cause it to take deep | root,..and it | filled the | land.

11 The hills were covered with the shadow of it,
And the boughs thereof were like the | good-ly | cedars.
12 She sent out her boughs unto the sea,
And her | branches..un-| to the | river.

13 Why hast thou then broken down her hedges,
So that all they which pass by the | way do | pluck her?
14 The boar out of the wood doth waste it,
And the wild | beast..of the | field..doth de-| vour it.

15 Return, we beseech thee, O God of hosts,
Look down from heaven, and behold, and | visit..this | vine;
16 And the vineyard which thy right hand planted,
And the branch that thou madest | strong for | thy — | self.

17 It is burnt with fire; it is cut down:
They perish at the rebuke of | thy — | countenance.
18 Let thy hand be upon the man of thy right hand,
Upon the son of man whom thou madest | strong for | thy — | self.

19 So will not we go back from thee:
Quicken us, and we will | call up..on thy | name.
20 Turn us again, O Lord God of hosts,
Cause thy face to | shine, and | we..shall be | saved.

1 As the hart panteth after the water-brook,
So panteth my soul after | thee, O | God.
2 My soul thirsteth for God, for the living God:
When shall I come and ap-| pear be-| fore — | God?

3 My tears have been my meat | day and | night,
4 While they continually say unto me,
| Where is | thy — | God?

5 When I remember these things,
I pour out my soul in me:
For I had | gone..with the | multitude:
6 I went with them to the house of God,
With the voice of joy and praise,
With a multitude that | kept — | holy | day.

7 Why art thou cast down, O my soul?
And why art thou dis-| quie..ted | in me?
8 Hope thou in God; for I shall yet praise him
For the | help of | his — | countenance.

---

9 O my God, my soul is cast | down with-| in me:
10 Therefore will I remember thee from the land of Jordan,
And of the Hermonites, | from the | hill — | Mizar.

11 Deep calleth unto deep at the noise of thy water-spouts:
All thy waves and thy billows are | gone — | over me.
12 Yet the Lord will command his loving kindness in the day time,
And in the night his song shall be with me,
And my prayer to the | God of | my — | life.

13 I will say unto God my rock, Why hast thou forgotten me?
Why go I mourning, because of the op-| pression..of the | enemy?
14 As with a sword in my bones, mine enemies reproach me.
While they say daily to me, | Where is | thy — | God?

15 Why art thou cast down, O my soul?
And why art thou dis-| quiet..ed with-| in me?
16 Hope thou in God; for I shall yet praise him,
Who is the health of my | counte-nance | and my | God.

SELECTION 62. [Ps. xciii.]

1 The Lord reigneth; he is clothed with majesty;
The Lord is clothed with strength,
Wherewith he hath | girded..him-| self;
2 The world also is established,|that it | cannot..be | moved.

3 Thy throne is established of old
Thou art from | ev-er-| lasting.
4 The floods have lifted up, O LORD,
The floods have lifted up their voice;
The | floods lift | up their | waves.

5 The Lord on high is mightier
Than the noise of many waters,
Yea, than the mighty | waves..of the | sea.
6 Thy testimonies are very sure;
Holiness becometh thine | house, O | Lord, for-| ever.

SELECTION 63. [Ps. xxxii. 1, 2, 5, 10 & 11.]

1 Blessed is he
Whose transgression is forgiven,
Whose | sin is | covered.
2 Blessed is the man
Unto whom the LORD imputeth not iniquity,
And in whose | spirit..there | is no | guile.

3 I acknowledged my sin unto thee,
And mine iniquity | have I..not | hid.
4 I said, "I will confess my transgressions unto the LORD:
And thou forgavest the in-| iqui ty | of my | sin. (SYM.)

5 Many sorrows shall be to the wicked;
But he that trusteth in the LORD,
Mercy shall encompass | him a-| bout.
6 Be glad in the LORD, and rejoice, ye righteous;
And shout for joy, all | ye..that are | upright..in | heart.

CHANT No. 38.

SELECTION 64. [Ps. xxxiv. 15–22.]

1 { The eyes of the LORD are upon the righteous,
And his ears are open un-| to their | cry.

2 { The face of the LORD is against them that do evil
To cut off the re-| membrance..of | them..from the | earth.

3 { The righteous cry, and the LORD heareth,
And delivereth them out of | all their | troubles.

4 { The LORD is nigh unto them that are of a broken heart,
And saveth such as | are..of a | contrite | spirit.

5 { Many are the afflictions of the righteous,
But the LORD delivereth him | out..of them | all.

6 { He keepeth all his bones;
Not | one of | them is | broken.

7 { Evil shall slay the wicked,
And they that hate the righteous | shall be | desolate.

8 { The LORD redeemeth the soul of his servants,
And none of them that | trust in | him..shall be | desolate.

CHANT No. 39.

SELECTION 65. [Ps. ciii. 8–14.]

1 { The LORD is merciful and gracious,
Slow to anger, and a-| bundant..in | mercy.

2 { He will not always chide;
Neither will he | keep his | anger..for-| ever.

3 { He hath not dealt with us after our sins,
Nor rewarded us according to | our in-| iquities.

4 { For as the heaven is high above the earth,
So great is his mercy toward | them that | fear— | him

5 { As far as the east is from the west,
So far hath he removed our trans-| gressions | from us.

6 { Like as a father pitieth his children,
So the LORD pitieth | them that | fear— | him.

7 { For he knoweth our frame;
He remembereth that | we are | dust.

8 { He knoweth our frame;
He remembereth, that | we, that | we are | dust.

CHANT No. 40.

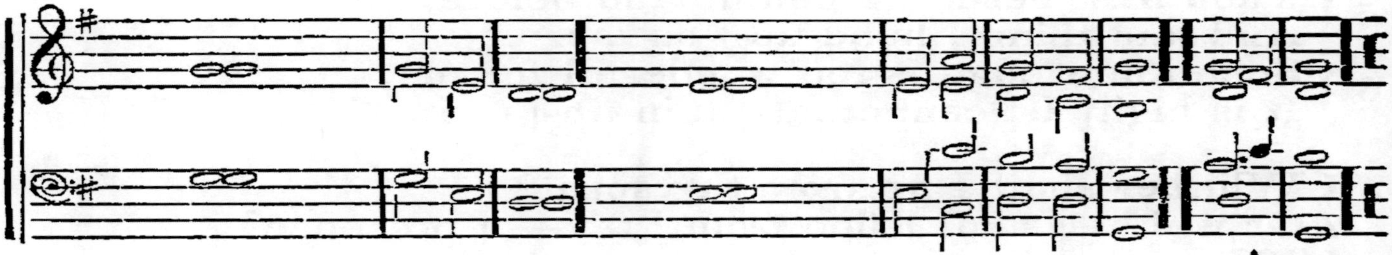

SELECTION 66. [Is. xxvi. 1–4.]

In that day shall this song be sung in the land of Judah;

1 { We have a strong city;
Salvation will God appoint for | walls and | bulwarks.

2 { Open ye the gates,
That the righteous nation which keepeth the | truth, may |
enter | in.

3 { Thou wilt keep him in perfect peace,
Whose mind is stayed on thee;
Because he | trusteth..in | thee.

4 { Trust ye in the LORD forever;
For in the LORD JEHOVAH is | ever-| lasting | strength.

CHANT No. 41.

SELECTION 67. [Ps. cxxxix.1–12, 23–24.]

1 O Lord, thou hast searched me, and | known— | me.

2 Thou knowest my down-sitting and mine up-rising;
Thou understandest my | thought a-| far— | off.

3 Thou compassest my path, and my lying down,
And art acquainted with | all my | ways.

4 For there is not a word on my tongue,
But lo, O Lord, thou | knowest..it | al-to-| gether.

5 Thou hast beset me behind and before,
And laid thine | hand up-| on me.

6 Such knowledge is too wonderful for me;
It is high, I | cannot..at-| tain un-| to it.

7 Whither shall I go from thy spirit?
Or whither shall I flee from | thy— | presence?

8 If I ascend into heaven, thou art there;
If I make my bed in | hell, be-| hold..thou art | there.

9 If I take the wings of the morning,
And dwell in the uttermost | parts..of the | sea;

10 Even there shall thy hand lead me,
And thy | right..hand shall | hold— | me.

11 If I say, Surely the darkness shall cover me;
Even the night shall be | light a-| bout me.

12 Yea, the darkness hideth not from thee;
But the night shineth as the day;
The darkness and the light are | both a-| like to | thee.

13 Search me, O God, and know my heart;
Try me, and | know my | thoughts;

14 And see if there be any wicked way in me,
And lead me in the | way, the | way..ever-| lasting.

SELECTION 68. [Ps.xc.13–17.]

1 Return, O Lord, how long?
And let it repent thee con-| cerning..thy | servants.

2 O satisfy us early with thy mercy;
That we may rejoice and be | glad all | our— | days.

3 Make us glad according to the days wherein thou hast afflicted us,
And the years wherein we have | seen — | evil.

4 Let thy work appear unto thy servants,
And thy | glory..un-| to their | children.

5 And let the beauty of the Lord our God be upon us;
And establish thou the work of our | hands up-| on us;

6 Yea, the work of our hands, es-| tablish | thou — | it.

CHANT No. 42.

SELECTION 69. [Ps. xxxvii. 35–39.]

1 I have seen the wicked in great power,
And spreading himself like a | green— | bay-tree.

2 Yet he passed away, and lo he was not;
Yea, I sought him, but | he could | not be | found.

3 Mark the perfect man, and behold the upright;
For the end of that | man is | peace.

4 But the transgressors shall be destroyed together,
The end of the | wicked..shall | be cut | off.

5 But the salvation of the righteous is of the Lord:
He is their strength in | time of | trouble.

6 And the Lord will help them, and deliver them;
He will deliver them from the wicked,
And save them, be-| cause they | trust in | him.

CHANT No. 43.

SELECTION 70. [Ps. xl. 11–17.]

1 Withhold not thou thy tender mercies from me,|O—|Lord:

2 Let thy loving kindness and thy | truth con-| tinual..ly
pre-| serve me.

3 For innumerable evils have encompassed me about;
Mine iniquities have taken hold upon me,
So that I am not | able..to look | up;

4 They are more than the hairs of my head;
Therefore my | heart, my | heart— | faileth me.

5 Be pleased, O Lord, to deliver me:
O Lord, make | haste to | help me.

6 O | Lord, make | haste to | help me.

7 Let them be ashamed and confounded together
That seek after my | soul..to de-| stroy it;

8 Let them be driven backward,
And put to | shame, that | wish me | evil.

9 Let them be desolate for a reward of their shame,
That say unto me, A-| ha, a-| ha!

10 Let all those that seek thee
Rejoice and be glad in thee;
Let such as love thy salvation say continually,
The | Lord be | magni-| fied.

11 But I am poor and needy;
Yet the Lord | thinketh..up-| on me.

12 Thou art my help and my deliverer:
Make no | tarry..ing | O my | God.

SELECTION 71. [Rev. xiv. 13.]

1 Blessed are the dead,
Who die in the | LORD from | henceforth:

2 Yea, saith the Spirit, that they may rest from their labors;
And their | works do | follow | them.

ch. xx. 6.

3 Blessed and holy is he that hath part in the first resurrection:
On such the second death | hath no | power;

4 But they shall be priests of God and of Christ,
And shall reign with | him a | thousand | years.

ch. I. 5.

5 Unto him that loved us,
And washed us from our sins in | his own | blood,

6 And hath made us kings and priests to God and his Father;
To him be glory and do-|minion..for-|ever and | ever.

SELECTION 72. [Ps. ciii. 15–18.]

1 As for man, his days are as grass;
As a flower of the field, | so he | flourisheth:

2 For the wind passeth over it, and it is gone;
And the place there-| of shall | know it..no | more.

3 But the mercy of the LORD is from everlasting
To everlasting upon them that fear him,
And his righteousness unto | chil-dren's | children;

4 To such as keep his covenant,
And to those that re-| member..his com-| mandments..to | *do* them.

CHANT No. 45.

SELECTION 73. [Habakkuk iii.]

1 O LORD, I have heard thy speech, and | was a-| fraid:
2 { O LORD, revive thy work in the midst of the years,
In the midst of the years make known;
In | wrath re-| member | mercy. (SYM.)

CHANT No. 46.

3 { God came from Teman,
And the Holy One from | mount— | Paran.
4 { His glory covered the heavens,
And the | earth was | full of..his | praise.

5 { And his brightness was as the light;
He had horns coming out of his hand;
And there was the | hiding..of his | power.
6 { Before him went the pestilence,
And burning | coals went | forth..at his | feet.

7 { He stood and measured the earth:
He beheld, and drove asunder the nations;
The everlasting mountains were scattered,
The perpetual | hills did | bow:
8 His | ways are | ever-| lasting.

9 { The mountains saw thee, and they trembled;
The deep uttered his voice, and lifted up his|hands on|high
10 { The sun and moon stood still in their habitation:
At the light of thine arrows they went,
And at the | shining..of thy | glitter-ing | spear.

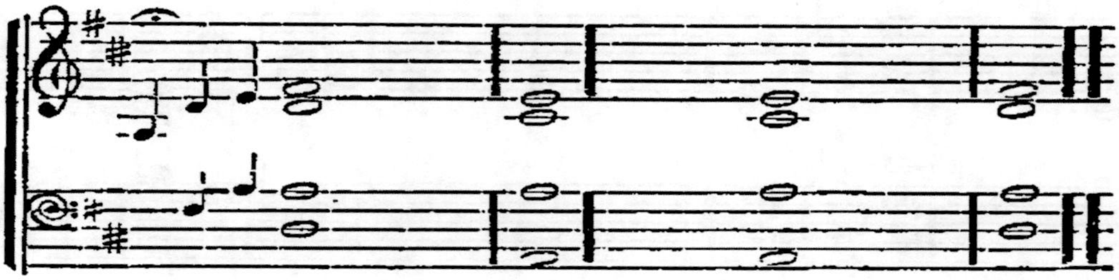

11 Although the fig-tree shall not blossom, neither shall
fruit be in the | vines;

12 The labor of the olive shall fail, and the fields shall yield
no | meat;

13 The flock shall be cut off from the fold, and there shall
be no herd in the | stalls:

14 Yet I will rejoice in the LORD,—I will joy in the God of
my sal-| vation.

SELECTION 74. [Ps. lxxvii. 16–20.]

1 The waters saw thee, O God, the waters saw thee;
They were afraid; the depths | also..were | troubled.

2 The clouds poured out water; the skies sent out a sound:
Thine | arrows..also | went a | broad.

3 The voice of thy thunder was in the heaven,
The lightnings | lightened..the | world:

4 The earth also trembled—
The | earth..also | trembled..and | shook.

5 Thy way is in the sea, and thy path in the great waters,
And thy footsteps | are not | known.

6 Thou leddest thy people like a flock,
By the | hand of | Moses..and | Aaron.

CHANT No. 48.

SELECTION 75. [Ps. cxviii.14,15,19,20,21,29.]

1 { The Lord is my strength and song,
And is become | my sal-| vation.

2 { The voice of rejoicing and salvation
Is in the tabernacles of the righteous:
The right | hand..of the | Lord..doeth | valiantly.

3 { Open to me the gates of righteousness:
I will go into them, and I will | praise the | Lord;

4 { This gate of the Lord,
Into | which the | righteous..shall | enter.

5 { I will praise thee; for thou hast heard me,
And art become | my sal-| vation.

6 { O give thanks unto the Lord, for he is good;
For his | mer..cy en-| dureth..for-| ever.

CHANT No. 49.

SELECTION 76. [Ps. cxviii. 22–29.]

1 { The stone which the builders refused
Is become the | head-stone..of the | corner.

2 { This is the Lord's doing;
It is | marvel..lous | in our | eyes.

3 { This is the day which the Lord hath made;
We will rejoice and be | glad in | it.

4 { Save now, I beseech thee, O Lord;
O Lord, I beseech thee, | send— | now pros-| perity.

5 { Blessed is he that cometh in the name of the LORD;
We have blessed you out of the | house..of the | LORD.

6 { God is the LORD which hath showed us light;
Bind the sacrifice with cords,
Even unto the | horns— | of the | altar.

7 { Thou art my God, and I will praise thee;
Thou art my God, | I..will ex-| alt thee.

8 { O give thanks unto the LORD, for he is good;
For his | mercy..en-| dureth..for-| ever.

CHANT No. 50.

SELECTION 77. [Ps. cxxvi.]

1 { When the LORD turned again the captivity of Zion,
We were like | them that | dream.

2 { Then was our mouth filled with laughter
And our | tongue broke | out with | singing.

3 { Then said they among the heathen,
The LORD hath done great | things for | them.

4 { The LORD hath done great things for | us,
Where-| of..we are | glad.

5 { Turn again our captivity, O LORD,
As the | streams..in the | south.

6 They that sow in tears shall | reap, shall | reap in | joy.

7 He that goeth forth weeping, | bearing..precious | seed,

8 { Shall, doubtless, come again with rejoicing,
| Bringing..his | sheaves— | with him.

CHANT No. 51.

SELECTION 78. [Ps. xliii.]

1 { Judge me, O God, and plead my cause
Against an un-| god-ly | nation;
2 O deliver me from the de-| ceitful and | unjust | man.

3 { For thou art the God of my strength;
Why dost thou | cast me | off?
4 Why go I mourning of the op-| pression | of the | enemy!

5 O send out thy | light..and thy | truth,
6 { Let them lead me, let them bring me
Unto thy holy | hill, and | to thy | tabernacles.

7 { Then will I go unto the altar of God,
Unto God my ex-| ceeding | joy;
8 Yea, upon the harp will I | praise thee..O|God, my|God.

9 { Why art thou cast down, O my soul?
And why art thou dis-| quiet..ed with-| in me?
10 { Hope thou in God; for I shall yet praise him,
Who is the health of my | counte..nance | and my | God.

CHANT No. 52.

SELECTION 79. [Ps. lvii. 5, 7–11.]

1 { Be thou exalted, O God, above the heavens;
Let thy glory be above | all the | earth.
2 { My heart is fixed, O God, my heart is fixed;
I will | sing and | give — | praise.

3 Awake up, my glory; awake psaltery and harp;
I myself will a-| wake — | early.

4 I will praise thee, O Lord, among the people;
I will sing unto | thee a-| mong the | nations.

5 For thy mercy is great unto the heavens,
And thy | truth un..to the | clouds.

6 Be thou exalted, O God, above the heavens;
Let thy glory be a-| bove all | — the | earth.

CHANT No. 53.

SELECTION 80. [From Ps. lxxii.]

1 He shall come down like rain upon the mown grass;
As showers that | wa-ter the | earth.

2 In his days shall the righteous flourish;
And abundance of peace as | long..as the | moon en-| dureth.

3 He shall judge the people with righteousness,
And the | poor with | judgment.

4 He shall have dominion also from sea to sea,
And from the | river..to the | ends..of the | earth.

5 His name shall endure forever:
His name shall be continued as | long..as the | sun;

6 And men shall be blessed in him:
All | na-tions shall | call him | blessed.

CHANT No. 54.

SELECTION 81. [Is. ix. 2, 6, 7: Luke ii. 14.]

1 { The people that walked in darkness,
Have | seen a..great | light;

2 { They that dwell in the land of the shadow of death,
Upon | them..hath the | light— | shined.

3 { For unto us a Child is born,
Unto us a Son is given;
And the government shall be up-| on his | shoulder;

4 { And his name shall be called Wonderful,
Counsellor, The Mighty God,
The Everlasting | Father..The | Prince of | Peace.

5 { Of the increase of his government and peace there shall be no end,
Upon the throne of David, and up-| on his | kingdom,

6 { To order it, and to establish it with judgment
And with justice, from|henceforth | even..for-| ever. (SYM.)

CHANT No. 55.

7 { Glory be to God in the highest,
And on earth peace, good | will to | men.

8 { Glory be to God in the highest,
And on earth | peace, good | will to | men

CHANT No. 56.

SELECTION 82. [Ps. lxxiii.]

1 Truly God is good to Israel,
Even to such as are of a | clean — | heart.

2 But as for me, my feet were almost gone;
My | steps had | well nigh | slipped.

3 For I was envious at the foolish,
When I saw the pros-| perity..of the | wicked.

4 For there are no bands in their death;
But their | strength, their | strength is | firm. (SYM.)

5 When I thought to know this,
It was too | painful | for me.

6 Until I went into the sanctuary of God;
| Then under-| stood..I their | end.

7 Surely thou didst set them in slippery places;
Thou castedst them | down..to de-| struction.

8 How are they brought into desolation, as in a moment!
They are | utterly..con-| sumed..with | terrors.

9 As a dream, when | one a-| waketh;

10 So, O Lord, when thou awakest,
| Thou..shalt de-| spise their | image.

11 For lo, they that are far from | thee shall | perish:

12 Thou hast destroyed all them that | go a-| stray from | thee.

13 But it is good for me to draw | near to | God;

14 I have put my trust in the Lord,
That I may de-| clare all | thy — | works.

CHANT No. 57.

SELECTION 83. [Joel 2. 1–3, 10-13.]

1 Blow ye the trumpet in Zion,
And sound an alarm in my | holy | mountain:
2 Let all the inhabitants of the land tremble;
For the day of the LORD | cometh..it is | nigh at | hand.

3 A day of darkness, and of gloominess,
A day of clouds and of thick darkness,
As the morning spread up-| on the | mountains;
4 A great people and a strong;
There hath not been ever the like,
Neither shall be any more after it,
Even to the | years of | many..gene-| rations.

5 A fire devoureth before them;
And behind them a | flame — | burneth:
6 The land is as the garden of Eden before them,
And be-| hind .them a | deso-late | wilderness.

7 The earth shall quake before them;
The | heavens..shall | tremble.
8 The sun and the moon shall be dark,
And the | stars..shall with-| draw their | shining.

9 And the LORD shall utter his voice before his army;
For his camp is very great:
For he is strong that | executeth..his | word:
10 For the day of the LORD is great and very terrible;
And | who — | who..can a-| bide it? (SUM.)

CHANT No. 58.

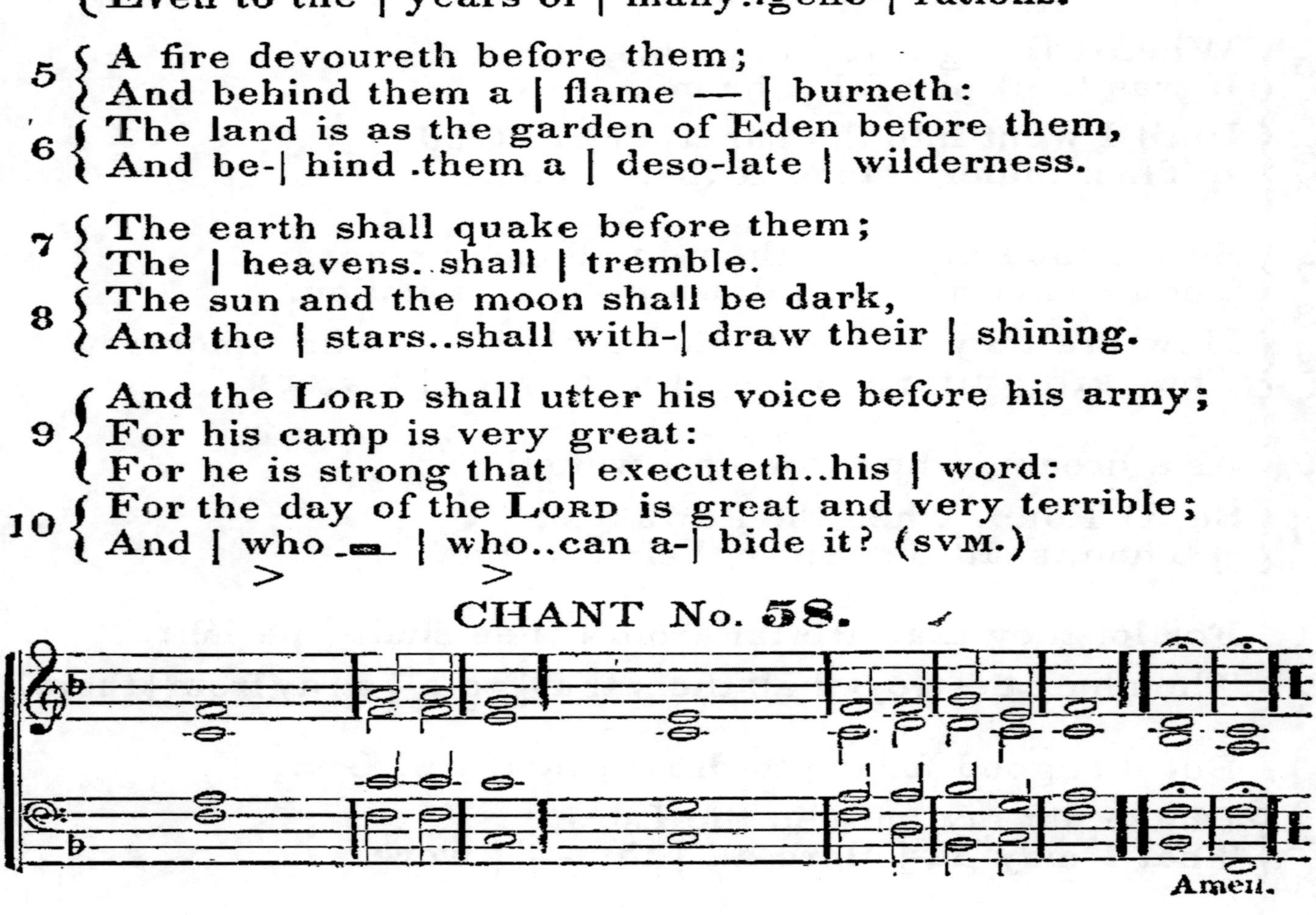

11 Therefore also now, saith the LORD,
Turn ye even to me with | all your | heart.
12 And with fasting, and with | weeping,..and with | mourning;

13 And rend your heart, and not your garments,
And turn unto the | LORD your | God;
14 For he is gracious and merciful,
Slow to anger, and of great kindness,
And re-| penteth..him | of the | evil.

CHANT No. 59.

SELECTION 84. [Ps. xxxvii. 1–6. 8, 9.]

1 Fret not thyself because of evil doers,
Neither be thou envious against the | workers..of in-| iquity.
2 For they shall soon be cut down like the grass,
And | wither..as the | green — | herb.

3 Trust in the LORD and do good,
So shalt thou dwell in the land, and verily thou | shalt be | fed.
4 Delight thyself also in the LORD,
And he shall give thee the de-| sires of | thine — | heart.

5 Commit thy way unto the LORD;
Trust also in him, and he shall | bring..it to | pass:
6 And he shall bring forth thy righteousness as the light.
And thy | judgment | as the | noon-day.

7 Cease from anger and forsake wrath;
Fret not thyself in any wise to | do — | evil.
8 For evil doers shall be cut off,
But those that wait upon the LORD, | they..shall in-| herit the | earth.

CHANT No. 60.

SELECTION 85. [Ezekiel xviii. 26.]

1 When a righteous man turneth away from his righteousness,
And committeth iniquity, and | dieth..in | them;

2 For his iniquity that he hath done, | shall — | he— | die.
(SYM.)

3 When the wicked man turneth away from his wickedness that he hath committed,
And doeth that which is | lawful..and | right,

4 He shall save his soul—
Shall | save his | soul a-| live.

5 Because he considereth, and turneth away from all his transgressions,
That | he..hath com-| mitted;

6 He shall surely live, | he shall | not — | die. (SYM.)

7 I will judge you, O house of Israel,
Every one according to his ways, | saith the..Lord | God.

8 Repent, and turn yourselves from all your transgressions,
So iniquity | shall not | be your | ruin.

9 Cast away from you all your transgressions,
Whereby ye | have trans-| gressed;

10 And make you a new heart and a new spirit:
For why will ye | die, O | house of | Israel?

11 For I have no pleasure in the death of him that dieth,
| Saith the. Lord | God;

12 Wherefore turn ye—
| Turn — | ye and | live.

SELECTION 86. [Ps. xxxiv. 9–14.]

1 O fear the LORD, ye his saints,
For there is no want to them that | fear — | him,
2 The young lions do lack, and suffer hunger;
But they that seek the LORD,
Shall | not want | any..good | thing.

3 Come, ye children, hearken unto me;
I will teach you the | fear..of the | LORD.
4 What man is he that desireth life,
And liveth many days, that | he may | see — | good.

5 Keep thy tongue from evil,
And thy lips from | speaking | guile.
6 Depart from evil, and do good;
| Seek — | peace..and pur-| sue it.

SELECTION 87. [Ps. xxv. 1–10.]

1 Unto thee, O LORD, do I lift | up my | soul:
2 O my God,
I trust in thee: let me not be asham'd;
Let not mine | ene-mies | triumph | over me.

3 Yea, let none that wait on thee be asham'd:
Let them be asham'd which trans-| gress with. out | cause.
4 Show me thy ways, O LORD;
| Teach me | thy — | paths.

5 Lead me in thy truth, and teach me:
For thou art the God of my salvation;
On thee do I wait | all the | day.
6 Remember, O LORD, thy tender mercies,
And thy loving kindness; for|they..have been|ever..of |old.

7 Remember not the sins of my youth, nor my transgressions;
According to thy mercy remember thou me,
For thy goodness' | sake, O | LORD.
8 Good and upright is the LORD;
Therefore will he teach | sinners | in the | way..

9 The meek will he guide in judgment:
And the meek will he | teach his | way.
10 All the paths of the LORD are mercy and truth,
Unto such as keep his | cove-nant | and his | testimonies.

CHANT No. 61.

SELECTION 88. [Ps. lxxxvii.]

1 His foundation is in the | holy | mountains.

2 The Lord loveth the gates of Zion
More than | all the | dwellings..of | Jacob.

3 Glorious things are spoken of thee, O | city..of | God.

4 Glorious things are spoken of thee, O|city, O|city..of |God.
(SYM.)

5 I will make mention of Rahab and Babylon
To them that know me;
Behold, Philistia, and Tyre, with Ethiopia;
This man was | born — | there.

6 And of Zion it shall be said,
This and that man was born in her;
And the Highest him-| self..shall es-| tablish | her.

7 The Lord shall count, when he writeth up the people,
That this man was | born — | there.

8 As well the singers as the players on instruments shall be there:
| All my | springs..are in | thee.

SELECTION 89. [From Ps. lxxxix.]

1 Blessed is the people that know the joyful sound:
They shall walk, O Lord, in the|light..of thy|countenance.

2 In thy name shall they rejoice all the day:
And in thy righteousness | shall they | be ex-| alted.

3 For thou art the glory of their strength;
And in thy favor our horn shall | be ex-| alted.

4 For the Lord is our defence;
And the Holy One of | Israel | is our | King.

CHANT No. 62.

SELECTION 90. [Ps. lxv. 8-13.]

1 Thou, LORD, makest the outgoings of the morning
And | evening..to re-| joice;

2 Thou visiteth the earth, and waterest it;
Thou greatly enrichest it with the river of | God..which is|
full of | water:

3 Thou preparest them corn,
When thou hast so pro-| vided | for it.

4 Thou waterest the ridges thereof abundantly;
Thou | settlest..the | furrows..there-| of:

5 Thou makest it soft with showers;
Thou blessest the | springing. there-| of.

6 Thou crownest the year with thy goodness:
And | thy paths | drop — | fatness.

7 They drop upon the pastures of the wilderness;
And the little hills rejoice on | every | side.

8 The pastures are clothed with flocks;
The vallies also are covered over with corn;
They shout for | joy, they | also | sing.

SELECTION 91. [From Ps. cxxxv.]

1 PRAISE YE THE LORD.
Praise ye the name of the LORD;
Praise him, O ye | servants..of the | LORD.

2 Ye that stand in the house of the LORD,
In the | courts..of the | house of..our | God.

3 Bless the LORD, O house of Israel:
Bless the LORD, O house of Aaron:
Bless the LORD, O house of Levi:
Ye that fear the LORD, | bless the | LORD.

4 Blessed be the LORD out of Zion,
Which dwelleth at Jerusalem.
| Praise — | ye the | LORD.

CHANT No. 63.

SELECTION 92. [Ps. cxxviii.]

1 Blessed is every one that feareth the LORD;
That walketh | in his | ways.
2 For thou shalt eat the labor of thine hands:
Happy shalt thou be, and it | shall be | well with | thee.

3 Thy wife shall be as a fruitful vine by the | side of..
thy | house:
4 Thy children like olive-plants,| round a-| bout thy | table.

5 Behold, that thus shall the man be blessed
That | feareth..the | LORD.
6 Thus shall the man be | blessed..that | feareth..the | LORD.

7 The LORD shall bless thee out of Zion:
And thou shalt see the good of Jerusalem all the | days..
of thy | life.
8 Yea, thou shalt see thy children's children,
And | peace up-| on — | Israel.

SELECTION 93. [Ps. xxv. 11–22.]

1 For thy name's sake, O LORD,
Pardon mine iniquity, for | it is | great.
2 What man is he that feareth the LORD?
Him shall he teach in the | way that | he shall | choose.

3 His soul shall dwell at ease;
And his seed shall in-| herit..the | earth.
4 The secret of the LORD is with them that fear him;
And he will | show — | them his | covenant.

5 Mine eyes are ever toward the LORD:
For he shall pluck my feet | out..of the | net.
6 Turn thee unto me, and have mercy upon me;
For I am | deso-late | and af-| flicted.

7 The troubles of my heart are enlarged:
O bring thou me out of | my dis-| tress.
8 Look upon mine affliction and my pain,
And for-| give all | my — | sins.

9 Consider mine enemies; for they are many;
And they hate me with | cruel | hatred.

10 O keep my soul, and deliver me:
Let me not be asham'd; for I | put my | trust in | thee.

11 Let integrity and uprightness preserve me;
For I | wait on | thee.

12 Redeem Israel, O God—
Redeem Israel out of | all — | his — | troubles.

CHANT No. 64.

SELECTION 94.

[Luke ii.]

1 There were shepherds abiding in the field,
Keeping watch over their | flock by | night.

2 And lo, the angel of the Lord came upon them,
And the glory of the Lord shone round about them,
And | they were | sore a-| fraid.

3 And the angel said unto them, Fear not;
For behold, I bring you good tidings
Of great joy, which shall be to | all — | people.

4 For unto you is born this day, in the city of David,
A | Savior,..who is | Christ the Lord.

5 And suddenly there was with the angel,
A multitude of the heavenly host, praising|God, and|saying:

6 Glory to God in the highest
And on earth | peace, good | will to | men.

7 Glory to God in the highest, and on earth peace,good will to man. A - men.

A

CHANT No. 65.

B

CHANT No. 66.

A

SELECTION 95.

[Ps. xlvi.]

1 God is our refuge and strength,
A very present | help in | trouble.

2 Therefore we will not fear, though the earth be removed,
And though the mountains be carried into the | midst —|
of the | sea.

A

3 Though the waters thereof | roar..and be | troubled.
4 Though the mountains |shake..with the |swelling..there-|of.

B

5 There is a river, the streams whereof
Shall make glad the | city..of | God;
6 The holy place of the tabernacle of the|Most—|——|High.

B

7 God is in the midst of her; she shall | not be | moved.
8 God shall help her, and | that —| right —| early.

A

9 The heathen raged, the kingdoms were moved;
He uttered his voice, the | earth —| melted.
10 The Lord of hosts is with us;
The God of | Jacob | is our | refuge.

A

11 Come behold the work of the Lord,
What desolations he hath | made..in the | earth.
12 He maketh wars to cease unto the end of the earth;
He breaketh the bow, and cutteth the spear in sunder;
He burneth the | chariot | in the | fire

B
13 Be still, and know that | I am | God.
14 { I will be exalted among the heathen,
And will be ex-| alted | in the | earth.

B
15 { The LORD of hosts is with us;
The God of Jacob | is our | refuge.
16 { The LORD of hosts is with us;
The God of | Jacob | is our | refuge.

CHANT No. 67.

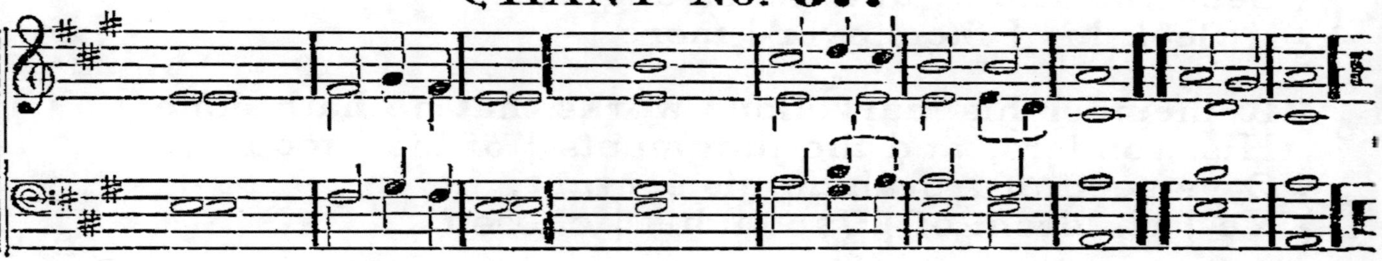

CHANT No. 68.

CHANT No. 69.

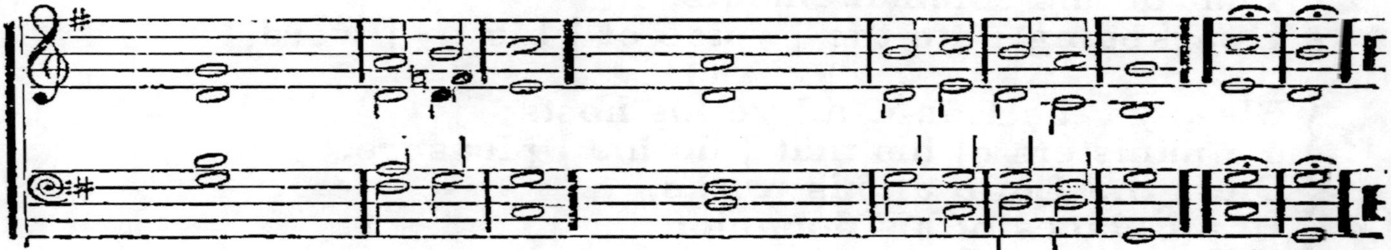

CHANT No. 70.

SELECTION 96. [Ps. cv. 1–6.]

1 O give thanks unto the Lord;
Call upon his name;
Make known his deeds a-|mong the | people.

2 Sing unto him, sing psalms unto him:
Talk ye of | all his | wondrous | works.

3 Glory ye in his holy name;
Let the heart of them rejoice, that | seek the | Lord.

4 Seek the Lord, and his strength;
| Seek his | face..ever-| more.

5 Remember his marvellous works that he hath done:
His wonders, and the judgments | of his | mouth;

6 O ye seed of Abraham his servant,
Ye | children..of | Jacob..his | chosen.

7 Glory ye in his holy name:
Let the heart of them rejoice that | seek the | Lord.

8 Seek the Lord, and his strength;
| Seek his | face..ever-| more.

SELECTION 97. [Ps. ciii. 19–22.]

1 The Lord hath prepared his throne in the heavens;
And his kingdom | ruleth..over | all.

2 Bless the Lord, ye his angels, that excel in strength,
That do his commandments,
Hearkening unto the | voice of | his — | word.

3 Bless ye the Lord, all ye his hosts;
Ye ministers of his that | do his | pleasure.

4 Bless the Lord all his works,
In all places of his dominion:
—Bless the | Lord..O my | soul.

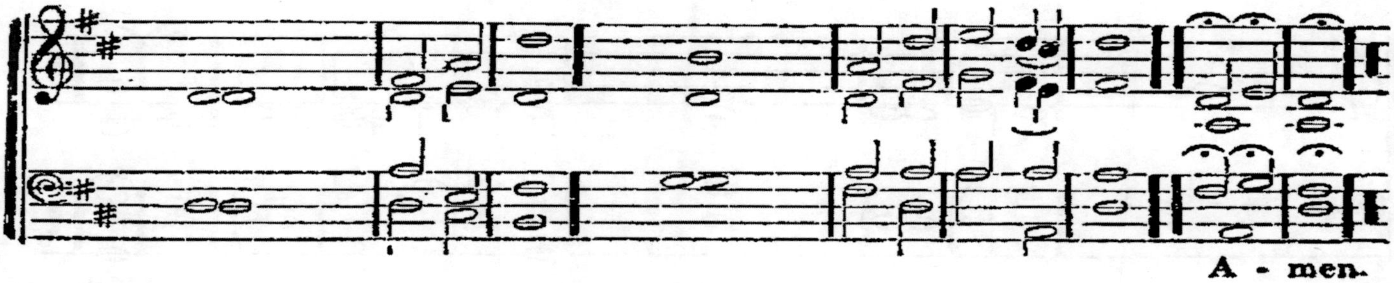

SELECTION 98. [From Ps. xxix]

1 Give unto the LORD, O ye mighty,
Give unto the LORD | glory..and | strength.
2 Give unto the LORD the glory due unto his name;
Worship the | LORD..in the | beauty..of | holiness.

3 The voice of the LORD is upon the waters:
The God of | glory | thundereth ;
4 The voice of the LORD is powerful
The voice of the | LORD is | full of | majesty.

5 The voice of the LORD breaketh the cedars;
Yea, the LORD breaketh the | cedars..of | Lebanon.
6 The voice of the LORD di-| videth..the | flames of | fire.

7 The voice of the LORD shaketh the wilderness;
And maketh | bare the | forests.
8 And in his temple doth | every..one | speak..of his | glory.

9 The LORD sitteth upon the flood;
Yea, the LORD sitteth | King for-| ever.
10 The LORD will give strength unto his people;
The LORD will | bless his | people..with | peace.

SELECTION 99. [Ps. ciii. 1–4.]

1 Bless the LORD, O my soul
And all that is within me, bless his | holy | name.
2 Bless the LORD, O my soul,
And for-| get not | all his | benefits.

3 Who forgiveth all thine iniquities;
Who healeth | all..thy dis-| eases;
4 Who redeemeth thy life from destruction;
Who crowneth thee with loving-| kindness..and | tender|
mercies.

SELECTION 100. [Ps. lxxxv. 8–12.]

1 { I will hear what God the LORD will speak,
For he will speak peace unto his people, and | to his | saints:
2 But let them not | turn a-| gain to | folly.

3 Surely his salvation is nigh | them that | fear him,
4 That | glory..may | dwell..in our | land.

5 { Mercy and truth are met together:
Righteousness and peace have | kissed..each | other.
6 { Truth shall spring out of the earth;
And righteousness shall look | down, look | down from |
heaven.

7 { Yea, the LORD shall give that which is good;
And our land shall | yield her | increase.
8 { Righteousness shall go before him,
And shall | set us..in the | way..of his | steps.

SELECTION 101. [Ps. xl. 1–4.]

1 { I waited patiently for the LORD,
And he inclined unto me, and | heard my | cry.
2 { He brought me up also out of an horrible pit,
Out of the miry clay,
And set my feet upon a rock,
And es-| tablish-ed | my — | goings.

3 { And he hath put a new song in my mouth,
Even praise un-| to our | God:
4 { Many shall see it, and fear,
And shall | trust, shall | trust..in the | LORD.

5 Blessed is that man that maketh the | LORD his | trust;
6 { And respecteth not the proud, nor such as | turn a-| side
to | lies.

SELECTION 102. [Ps. xxxiv. 1–8.]

The following Selections may be sung to any appropriate Chant.

1 { I will bless the LORD at all times;
His praise shall continually | be in..my | mouth.
2 { My soul shall make her boast in the LORD;
The humble shall | hear there-| of..and be | glad.

3 { O magnify the LORD with me,
And let us exalt his | name to-| gether.
4 { I sought the LORD, and he heard me,
And de-| livered..me from | all my | fears.

5 { They looked unto him and were lightened;
And their faces were | not a-| shamed.
6 { This poor man cried, and the LORD heard him,
And | saved him..out of | all his | troubles.

7 { The angel of the LORD encampeth
Around them that fear him, and de-| liver-eth | them.
8 { O taste and see that the LORD is good:
Blessed is the | man that | trusteth..in | him.

SELECTION 103. [Ps. lxxviii. 1–7.]

1 Give ear, O my people, | to my | law;
2 Incline your | ears..to the | words..of my | mouth.

3 { I will open my mouth in a parable;
I will utter dark | sayings..of | old;
4 { Which we have heard and known,
And our | fathers..have | told — | us.

5 { We will not hide them from their children,
Showing to the generation to come, the | praises..of the |
LORD.
6 And his strength, and his wonderful | works that | he hath | done.

7 { For he established a testimony in Jacob,
And appointed a | law in | Israel;
8 { Which he commanded our fathers,
That they should make them | known to | their — | children.

9 { That the generation to come might know them,
Even the children which | should be | born.
10 { Who should arise and declare them to *their* children:
That they might | set their | hope in | God.

SELECTION 104. [Ps. xlviii 1–3. 9-14.]

1 Great is the LORD, and greatly to be praised,
In the city of our God, in the | mountain..of his | holiness.

2 Beautiful for situation,
The joy of the whole | earth is | Mount — | Zion.

3 On the sides of the north, the city of the | great— | King.

4 God is known in her | pala-| ces | for a | refuge.

5 We have thought of thy loving-kindness,
O God in the | midst..of thy | temple.

6 According to thy name, O God,
So is thy praise unto the ends of the earth:
Thy right | hand is | full of | righteousness.

7 Let Mount Zion rejoice,
Let the daughters of Judah be glad,
Be-| cause of..thy | judgments.

8 Walk about Zion, and go round about her:
| Tell..ye the | towers there-| of.

9 Mark ye well her bulwarks, consider her palaces;
That ye may tell it to the gene-| ra-tion | following.

10 For this God is our God, for ever and ever;
He will be our | guide..even | unto | death.

SELECTION 105. [From Ps. lxxvii.]

1 I will remember the years of the right hand of the Most High:
I will remember the | works..of the | LORD.

2 Surely I will remember thy wonders—thy | won— | ders of | old.

3 I will meditate also of all thy work,
And talk of | thy — | doings.

4 Thy way, O God, is in the sanctuary:
Who is so | great a | God as | *our* God:

5 Thou art the God that doest wonders:
Thou hast declared thy strength a-| mong the | people.

6 Thou hast with thine arm redeemed thy people,
The | sons of | Jacob..and | Joseph.

SELECTION 106. [Ps. lxii. 5–12.]

1 { My soul, wait thou only upon God:
For my expectation | is from | him.

2 { He only is my rock and my salvation;
He is my defence; | I shall | not be | moved.

3 { In God is my salvation and my glory;
The rock of my strength, and my | refuge..is in | God.

4 { Trust in him at all times, ye people!
Pour out your heart before him:
| God..is a | refuge | for us.

5 { Surely men of low degree are vanity;
And men of high de-| gree..are a | lie:

6 { To be laid in the balance,
They are | alto-gether | lighter..than | vanity.

7 Trust not in oppression, and become not|vain in | robbery;
8 If riches increase, set | not your | heart up-| on them.

9 { God hath spoken once;
Twice have I heard this, that power be-|longeth..unto|God.

10 { Also unto thee, O Lord, belongeth mercy;
For thou renderest to every man ac-|cording | to his|work.

SELECTION 107. [Ps. xlvii and xli.]

1 { O clap your hands all ye people;
Shout unto God with the | voice of | triumph:

2 { For the Lord most high is terrible;
He is a great | King..over | all the | earth.

3 { He shall subdue the people under us,
And the nations | under..our | feet.

4 { He shall choose our inheritance for us,
The excellency of | Jacob..whom | he — | loved.

5 { Blessed be the Lord God of Israel,
From everlasting, and to | ev-er-| lasting.

6 A — | men, and | A — | men.

SELECTION 108. [From Ps. lxx.]

1 Make haste, O God, to deliver me;
Make haste to help me, | O — | LORD

2 Let them be ashamed and confounded
That | seek — | after..my | soul;

3 Let them be turned backward, and put to confusion
That de-| sire my | hurt.

4 Let them be turned back for a reward of their shame,
That | say, A-| ha, a-| ha!

5 Let all those that seek thee rejoice, and be | glad in|thee.

6 And such as love thy salvation
Say continually, Let | God be | magni-| fied.

7 But I am poor and needy;
Make haste unto me, | O — | God:

8 Thou art my help and my deliverer,
O | LORD, make | no de-| lay.

SELECTION 109. [Ps. lxxxi. 1–4.]

1 Sing aloud unto God our strength;
Make a joyful noise unto the | God of | Jacob.

2 Take a psalm, and bring hither the timbrel,
The pleasant | harp, the | harp..with the | psaltery.

3 Blow up the trumpet in the new moon;
In the time appointed, on our | solemn | feast-day;

4 For this was a statute for Israel:
And a | law..of the | God of | Jacob.

SELECTION 110. [Ps. xli. 1-3.]

1 Blessed is he that con-| sidereth..the | poor;
2 The LORD will de-| liver..him in | time of | trouble.

3 The LORD will preserve him, and | keep..him a-| live;
4 And he shall be | blessed..up-| on the | earth.

5 The LORD will strengthen him upon the|bed of|languishing;
6 Thou wilt make | all his | bed..in his | sickness.

SELECTION 111. [Ps. lxxxix. 7–14]

1 God is greatly to be feared in the assembly of the saints,
And to be had in reverence of all them that | are a-| bout him.

2 O LORD God of hosts, who is a strong LORD like unto thee?
Or to thy | faithful..ness | round a-| bout thee?

3 Thou rulest the raging of the sea:
When the waves thereof a-| rise, thou | stillest them:

4 Thou hast broken Rahab in pieces, as one that is slain:
Thou hast scattered thine | enemies..with | thy strong | arm.

5 The heavens are thine, the earth also is thine:
As for the world, and the fulness thereof, | thou hast | founded them.

6 The north and the south, thou hast created them;
Tabor and Hermon shall re-| joice in | thy — | name.

7 Thou hast a mighty arm:
Strong is thy hand, and | high..is thy | right hand.

8 Justice and judgment are the habitation of thy throne;
Mercy and truth shall | go be-| fore thy | face.

SELECTION 112. [Ps. lxxxvi. 8–12.]

1 All nations whom thou hast made
Shall come and worship before thee, | O — | LORD.

2 And shall | glori- fy | thy — | name.

3 For thou art great, and doest | wondrous | things,

4 Thou art God alone—
| Thou art | God a-| lone.

5 Teach me thy way, | O — | LORD;

6 I will walk in thy truth:
Unite my | heart to | fear thy | name.

7 I will praise thee, O LORD my God, with | all my | heart;

8 And I will glorify thy | name for-| ev-er | more.

SELECTION 113. [Ps. lxxii. 18–19.]

1 Blessed be the LORD GOD, the God of Israel;
Who only doeth | wondrous | things.

2 And blessed be his glorious name forever;
And let the whole earth be filled with his glory
A-| men, and | A —— | men.

1 O sing unto the LORD a new song;
For he hath done | marvel..lous | things:

2 His right hand and his holy arm, hath | gotten..hath |
gotten..him the | victory.

3 The LORD hath made known his salvation:
His righteousness hath he openly showed in the | sight..
of the | heathen.

4 He hath remembered his mercy and his truth
Toward the house of Israel:
And all the ends of the earth have seen the sal-| vation |
of our | God.

---

5 Make a joyful noise unto the LORD, all the earth;
Make a loud noise, and rejoice, and | sing — | praise.

6 Sing unto the LORD with the harp;
With the | harp..and the | voice..of a | psalm.

7 With trumpets, and sound of cornet,
Make a joyful noise before the | LORD the | King.

8 Let the sea roar, and the fullness thereof;
The world, and | they that | dwell there-| in.

9 Let the floods clap their hands:
Let the hills be joyful together, be-| fore the | LORD.

10 For he cometh to judge the earth:
With righteousness shall he judge the world,
And the | peo — | ple with | equity.

SELECTION 115. [Ps. xxviii. 6–9.]

1 Blessed be the LORD,
Because he hath heard the voice of my | sup-pli-| cations.

2 The LORD is my strength and my shield:
Therefore my heart greatly rejoiceth,
And with my | song will | I — | praise him.

3 The LORD is their strength,
And he is the saving strength of | his an-| ointed.

4 Save thy people, and bless thine inheritance:
Feed them also, and | lift them | up for-| ever.

SELECTION 116. [Ps. cvii. 23–32.]

1 { They that go down to the sea in ships,
That do business in | great — | waters;
2 { These see the works of the LORD,
And his | wonders | in the | deep.

3 { For he commandeth, and raiseth the stormy wind,
Which lifteth up the | waves there-| of.
4 { They mount up to the heaven,
They go down again to the depths;
Their soul is | melted..be | cause of | trouble.

5 { They reel to and fro, and stagger like a drunken man,
And are | at their..wit's | end.
6 { Then they cry unto the LORD in their trouble,
And he bringeth them | out of | their dis-| tresses.

7 { He maketh the storm a calm,
So that the waves there-| of are | still.
8 { Then are they glad because they be quiet;
So he bringeth them unto | their de-| sired | haven.

9 { Oh that men would praise the LORD for his goodness,
And for his wonderful works to the | children..of | men.
10 { Let them exalt him in the congregation of the people,
And praise him in the as-| sembly | of the | elders.

SELECTION 117. [From Ps. cvi.]

1 { Who can utter the mighty acts of the LORD?
Who can show forth | all his | praise?
2 { Blessed are they that keep judgment,
And he that doeth | righteous-| ness at | all times.

3 { Remember me, O LORD, with the favor
That thou bearest unto thy people:
O visit me with | thy sal-| vation.
4 { That I may see the good of thy chosen,
That I may rejoice in the gladness of thy nation,
That I may | glory..with | thine in-| heritance.

5 { Blessed be the LORD God of Israel from everlasting to
everlasting:
And let all the people | say, A-| men.
6 { Praise ye the LORD—
| Praise — | ye the | LORD.

SELECTION 118. [Ps. cxix. 41–48.]

1 Let thy mercies come unto me, O LORD;
Even thy salvation, ac-| cording..to thy | word.
2 So shall I have wherewith to answer him that reproacheth me:
For I | trust in | thy — | word.

3 And take not thy word utterly out of my mouth;
For I have | hoped..in thy | judgments.
4 So shall I keep thy law,
Con-| tinually..for-| ever and | ever.

5 And I will walk at liberty:
For I | seek thy | precepts.
6 I will speak of thy testimonies also before kings,
And | will not | be a-| shamed.

7 And I will delight myself in thy commandments,
Which | I have | loved.
8 My hands also will I lift up unto thy commandments, which I have loved;
And I will | medi-tate | in thy | statutes.

SELECTION 119. [Ps. cxix. 57–64.]

1 Thou art my portion, O LORD:
I have said that I would | keep thy | words.
2 I entreated thy favor with my whole heart:
Be merciful unto me ac-| cording | to thy | word.

3 I thought on my ways,
And turned my feet | unto..thy | testimonies.
4 I made haste and delayed not
To | keep — | thy com-| mandments.

5 The bands of the wicked have robbed me,
But I have not for-| gotten..thy | law.
6 At midnight I will rise to give thanks unto thee,
Be-| cause of..thy | righteous | judgments.

7 I am a companion of all them that fear thee,
And of them that | keep thy | precepts.
8 The earth, O LORD, is full of thy mercy:
| Teach — | me thy | statutes.

SELECTION 120. [Ps. cxix. 97–104.]

1 O how I love thy law!
It is my meditation | all the | day.
2 Thou, through thy commandments, hast made me wiser than mine enemies;
For | they are | ev-er | with me.

3 I have more understanding than all my teachers;
For thy testimonies are my | med-i-| tation.
4 I understand more than the ancients;
Be-| cause I | keep thy | precepts.

5 I have refrained my feet from every evil way,
That I might | keep thy | word.
6 I have not departed from thy judgments,
For | thou, for | thou hast | taught me.

7 How sweet are thy words unto my taste!
Yea, sweeter than honey | to my | mouth.
8 Through thy precepts I get understanding:
Therefore I | hate..every | false — | way.

SELECTION 121. [Ps. cxix. 169–176.]

1 Let my cry come near before thee, O Lord:
Give me understanding according | to thy | word.
2 Let my supplication come before thee:
Deliver me ac-| cor-ding | to thy | word.

3 My lips shall utter thy praise,
When thou hast | taught me..thy | statutes.
4 My tongue shall speak of thy word:
For | all..thy com-| mandments..are | righteousness.

5 Let thine hand help me;
For I have | chosen..thy | precepts.
6 I have longed for thy salvation, O Lord;
And thy | law is | my de-| light.

7 Let my soul live, and it shall praise thee;
And let thy | judgments | help me.
8 I have gone astray like a lost sheep:
Seek thy servant: for I do | not for-| get..thy com-| mandments.

SELECTION 122. [Ps. cxix. 1–8.]

1 { Blessed are the undefiled in the way
{ Who walk in the | law..of the | LORD.

2 { Blessed are they that keep his testimonies,
{ And that | seek him | with the..whole | heart.

3 { They also do no iniquity
{ They | walk in..his | ways

4 { Thou hast commanded us to keep thy precepts,
{ To | keep thy | pre-cepts | diligently.

5 { O that my ways were directed
{ To | keep thy | statutes.

6 { Then shall I not be ashamed
{ When I have res-| pect unto | all..thy com-| mandments.

7 { I will praise thee with uprightness of heart,
{ When I shall have learned thy | righteous | judgments.

8 { I will keep thy statutes,
{ | O for-| sake me..not | utterly.

SELECTION 123. [Ps. cxix. 9–16.]

1 { Wherewithal shall a young man cleanse his way?
{ By taking heed thereto accor-ding | to thy | word.

2 { With my whole heart have I sought thee.
{ O let me not | wander..from | thy com-| mandments

3 { Thy word have I hid in mine heart,
{ That I might not | sin a-| gainst thee.

4 { Blessed art thou, O LORD;
{ | Teach — | me thy | statutes.

5 { With my lips have I declared
{ All the judgments | of thy | mouth.

6 { I have rejoiced in the way of thy testimonies
{ As | much as | in all | riches,

7 { I will meditate in thy precepts,
{ And have respect | unto..thy | ways

8 { I will delight myself in thy statutes:
{ I will | not for-| get thy | word.

SELECTION 124. [Ps. cxix. 25–32.]

1 My soul cleaveth unto the dust;
Revive thou me according | to thy | word.

2 I have declared my ways, and thou heardest me:
| Teach — | me thy | statutes.

3 Make me to understand the way of thy precepts:
So shall I talk of thy | wondrous | works.

4 My soul melteth for heaviness:
Strengthen thou me, ac-| cor-ding | unto..thy | word.

5 Remove from me the way of lying;
And grant me thy | law — | graciously.

6 I have chosen the way of truth:
Thy | judgments..have I | laid be-| fore me.

7 I have adhered to thy testimonies;
O LORD, put me | not to | shame.

8 I will run the way of thy commandments
When | thou..shalt en-| large my | heart.

SELECTION 125. [Ps. cxix. 33–40.]

1 Teach me, O LORD, the way of thy statutes,
And I shall keep it | unto the | end.

2 Give me understanding, and I shall keep thy law;
Yea, I shall ob-| serve it..with | my whole | heart.

3 Make me to go in the path of thy commandments:
For therein do | I de-| light.

4 Incline my heart unto thy testimonies,
And | not, and | not to | covetousness.

5 Turn away mine eyes from beholding vanity;
And revive thou | me in..thy | way.

6 Establish thy word unto thy servant,
Who is de-| vo-ted | to thy | fear.

7 Turn away my reproach which I fear;
For thy | judgments..are | good.

8 Behold, I have longed after thy precepts:
Re-| vive me | in thy | righteousness.

SELECTION 126. [Ps. c.]

1 Make a joyful noise unto the LORD, | all..ye | lands.
2 { Serve the LORD with gladness;
Come before his | presence | with a | song.

3 Know ye that the LORD, | he is | God:
4 { It is he that hath made us, and not we ourselves.
We are his | people..and the | sheep..of his | pasture.

5 { Enter into his gates with thanksgiving,
And into his | courts with | praise:
6 Be thankful unto | him, and | bless his | name.

7 For the LORD is good, his mercy is | ever-| lasting.
8 And his truth endureth to | all — | gene-| rations.

SELECTION 127. [Ps. civ. 31–35.]

1 { The glory of the LORD shall endure forever:
The LORD shall re-| joice..in his | works.
2 { He looketh on the earth and it trembleth;
He toucheth the | hills, and | they — | smoke.

3 { I will sing unto the LORD as long as I live;
I will sing praise to my God while I | have my | being.
4 { My meditation of him shall be sweet:
I will be | glad, be | glad..in the | LORD:

5 { Let sinners be consumed out of the earth,
And let the wicked | be no | more.
6 { Bless thou the LORD, O my soul.
| Praise — | ye the | LORD.

SELECTION 128. [Ps. li. 15–18.]

1 { O LORD, open thou my lips;
And my mouth shall show | forth thy | praise.
2 { For thou desirest not sacrifice, else would I give it,
Thou delightest | not in | burnt — | offering.

3 { The sacrifices of God are a broken spirit;
A broken and a contrite heart,
O God, thou wilt | not des-| pise
4 { Do good in thy good pleasure unto Zion,
Build | thou the | walls..of Je-| rusalem.

SELECTION 129. [Is. i. 2–3.]

1 Hear, O heavens, and give ear, O earth;
For the | LORD hath | spoken;
2 I have nourished and brought up children,
And | they..have re-| belled..a-| gainst me.

3 The ox knoweth his owner, and the ass his | master's | crib:
4 But Israel doth not know, my | people..doth | not con-| sider.

Is. 1. 16–18.

5 Wash you, | make you | clean;
6 Put away the evil of your | doings..from be-| fore mine | eyes;

7 Cease to do evil: | Learn to..do | well:
8 Seek judgment, relieve the oppressed,
Judge the fatherless, | plead — | for the | widow.

9 Come now, and let us reason together,
| Saith the | LORD:
10 Though your sins be as scarlet, they shall be white as snow;
Though they be red like | crimson,..they shall | be as | wool.

SELECTION 130. [Is. ii. 5, 10, 11, 12 & 17.]

1 O house of Jacob, Come ye,
And let us walk in the | light..of the | LORD.
2 Enter into the rock, and hide thee in the dust,
For fear of the LORD, and for the | glory..of | his — | majesty.

3 The lofty looks of man shall be humbled,
And the haughtiness of men shall be | bowed | down;
4 And the LORD alone shall be ex-| alted..in | that — | day.

5 For the day of the LORD of hosts
Shall be upon every one that is | proud and | lofty;
6 And upon every high one that is lifted up,
And | he..shall be | brought — | low.

7 And the loftiness of man shall be bowed down,
And the haughtiness of men shall be | made — | low;
8 And the LORD alone shall be exalted—
Shall be ex-| alted..in | that — | day.

SELECTION 131. [Is. xii.]

And in that day thou shalt say,—
1 O LORD, I will praise thee;
| I will | praise thee:
2 Though thou wast angry with me,
Thine anger is turned away,
And | thou hast | comfort-ed | me.

3 Behold, God is my salvation;
I will trust, and | not..be a-| fraid;
4 For the LORD JEHOVAH is my strength and my song;
He also is be-| come — | my sal-| vation.

5 Therefore with joy shall ye draw water
Out of the | wells..of sal-| vation.
6 Praise the LORD, call upon his name,
Declare his doings among the people,
Make mention that | his name | is ex-| alted.

7 Sing unto the LORD; for he hath done excellent things;
This is known in | all the | earth.
8 Cry out and shout, thou inhabitant of Zion:
For great is the Holy One of | Israel..in the | midst of | thee.

SELECTION 132. [Is. xl. 1-5.]

1 Comfort ye, comfort ye my people, | saith your | God.
2 Comfort ye, comfort ye my | people, | saith your | God.

3 Speak ye comfortably to Jerusalem, and cry unto her,
That her warfare is accomplished, that her in-| iqui-ty
is | pardoned:
4 For she hath received of the LORD's hand | double..for |
all her | sins.

5 The voice of him that crieth in the wilderness,
Prepare ye the | way..of the | LORD,
6 Make straight in the desert a | highway..for | our — | God.

7 Every valley shall be exalted,
And every mountain and hill shall be | made — | low:
8 And the crooked shall be made straight,
And the | rough — | places | plain.

9 And the glory of the LORD shall be revealed,
And all flesh shall | see it..to-| gether,
10 For the | mouth..of the | LORD hath | spoken it.

1 The wilderness, and the solitary place, shall be glad;
And the desert shall rejoice, and | blossom..as the | rose.
2 It shall blossom abundantly,
And re-| joice..ev'n with | joy and | singing.

3 The glory of Lebanon shall be given unto it,
The excellency of | Carmel .and | Sharon;
4 They shall see the glory of the LORD,
And the | excellency..of | our — | God.

5 Strengthen ye the weak hands,
And confirm the | feeble | knees.
6 Say to them that are of a fearful heart,
Be strong, fear not; behold, your God will come with a recompense;
| He will | come and | save you.

7 Then the eyes of the blind shall be opened,
And the ears of the deaf shall | be un-| stopp'd:
8 Then shall the lame man leap as an hart,
And the | tongue..of the | dumb shall | sing;

9 For in the wilderness shall waters break out,
And | streams..in the | desert:
10 And the parched ground shall become a pool,
And the | thirsty..land | springs of | water.

11 In the habitation of dragons, where each lay,
Shall be grass, with | reeds and | rushes;
12 And a highway shall be there, and a way,
And it shall be called, The | way, the | way of | holiness;

13 The unclean shall | not pass | over it;
14 But it shall be for those;
The way-faring men, though | fools..shall not | err there-| in.

15 No lion shall be there, nor any ravenous beast shall go up thereon,
It shall | not be..found | there:
16 The redeemed of the | LORD shall | walk — | there.

17 And the ransomed of the LORD shall return,
And come to Zion with songs, and everlasting joy shall be up-| on their | heads:
18 They shall obtain joy and gladness,
And sorrow and | sighing..shall | flee a-| way.

SELECTION 134. [Is. xl. 28–31.]

1 Hast thou not known, hast thou not heard,
That the everlasting God, the LORD,
The Creator of the ends of the earth, fainteth not, |
neither..is | weary?
2 There is no | searching of | his..under-| standing.

3 He giveth power to the faint;
And to them that have no might he in-| creaseth | strength.
4 To them that have no | might..he in | creaseth | strength.

5 Even the youths shall faint and be weary,
And the young men shall | utter-ly | fall:
6 But they that wait upon the LORD,
Shall re-| new..shall re-| new their | strength:

7 They shall mount up with wings as eagles;
They shall run and | not be | weary,
8 And they shall | walk and | not — | faint.

SELECTION 135. [Is. xli. 10, 13, 14.]

1 Fear thou not; for I am with thee;
Be not dismayed, for | I am..thy | God:

2 I will strengthen thee; yea, I will help thee;
Yea, I will uphold thee with the right | hand of | my— |
righteousness.

3 For I the LORD thy God will hold thy right hand,
Saying unto thee, Fear not; | I will | help thee.
4 Fear not, thou worm Jacob, and ye men of Israel;
I will help thee, saith the LORD, and thy Redeemer,
The | Holy | One of | Israel.

SELECTION 136. [Is. xlii. 10, 11, & 12.]

1 Sing unto the LORD a new song,
And his praise from the | end..of the | earth,
2 Ye that go down to the sea, and all that is therein:
The | isles,..and th' in-| habitants..there-| of.

3 Let the wilderness and the cities thereof lift up their voice,
The villages that | Kedar..doth in-| habit:
4 Let the inhabitants of the rock sing,
Let them | shout..from the | top..of the | mountains.

5 Let them give glory unto the LORD,
And declare his | praise .in the | islands.
6 Let them give glory unto the LORD,
And de-| clare his | praise..in the | islands.

1 Thus saith the LORD that created thee, O Jacob,
And he that formed thee, O Israel, | Fear — | not:
2 For I have redeemed thee,
I have called thee by thy name; | thou — | art — | mine.

3 When thou passest through the waters, I will be with thee;
And through the rivers, they shall | not..over-| flow thee:
4 When thou walkest through the fire thou shalt not be burnt,
Neither shall the | flame — | kindle..up-| on thee.

5 For I am the LORD thy God,
The Holy one of | Israel..thy | Savior.
6 I gave Egypt for thy ransom,
Ethi-| opia..and | Seba | for thee.

7 Since thou wast precious in my sight,
Thou hast been honorable, and | I have | loved thee:
8 Therefore will I give men for thee,
And | people..for | thy — | life.

9 Fear not;
For | I am | with thee;
10 I will bring thy seed from the east,
And | gather..thee | from the | west.

11 I will say to the north, Give up;
And to the south, | Keep not | back;
12 Bring my sons from far,
And my | daughters..from the | ends..of the | earth.

13 I, even I, am the LORD;
And besides me there is | no — | Savior.
14 I am the LORD, your Holy one,
The Creator of | Israel, | your — | King.

15 I, even I, am he that blotteth out thy transgressions
For mine | own — | sake,
16 And will | not re-| member..thy | sins.

SELECTION 138. [Is. xliv. 2–6. 22.]

1 { Thus saith the LORD that made thee,
And formed thee, | which will | help thee;
2 { Fear not, O Jacob my servant;
And thou, | Jesurun,..whom | I have | chosen.

3 { For I will pour water upon him that is thirsty,
And floods upon the | dry — | ground;
4 { I will pour my spirit upon thy seed,
And my | blessing..up-| on thine | offspring:

5 { And they shall spring up as among the grass,
As willows by the | water- | courses.
6 { They shall spring up as among the grass,
As | willows..by the | water- | courses.

7 { One shall say, I am the LORD's;
And another shall call himself by the | name of | Jacob;
8 { And another shall subscribe with his hand unto the LORD,
And surname him-| self..by the | name of | Israel.

9 { Thus saith the LORD, the King of Israel,
And his Redeemer the | LORD of | hosts;
10 { I am the first, and I am the last;
And besides | me..there is | no — | God.

11 { Look unto me, and be ye saved,
All the | ends..of the | earth.
12 { Look unto me, and be ye saved,—
| All the | ends..of the | earth.

SELECTION 139. [Is. xlix. 13. & li. 3.]

1 { Sing, O heavens; and be joyful O earth;
And break forth into | singing..O | mountains;
2 { For the LORD hath comforted his people,
He will have | mercy..on | his af-| flicted.

3 { The LORD shall comfort Zion:
He will comfort | all her | waste places,
4 { He will make her wilderness like Eden,
And her | desert..like the | garden..of the | LORD.

5 { Joy and gladness shall be found therein,
Thanksgiving, and the | voice of | melody.
6 { Joy and gladness shall be found therein,
| Thanksgiving,..and the | voice of | melody:

SELECTION 140. [Is. lii. 1–2. & lv. 12-13.]

1 Awake, awake; put on thy strength, O Zion;
Put on thy beautiful garments, O Jerusalem, the | holy |
city:
2 For henceforth there shall no more come into thee,
The un-| circum..cised | and..th' un-| clean.

3 Shake thyself from the dust;
Arise, and sit down, | O Je-| rusalem:
4 Loose thyself from the bands of thy neck,
O | captive | daughter..of | Zion.

5 For ye shall go out with joy, and be led | forth in | peace:
6 The mountains and the hills shall break forth before you
into singing,
And all the trees of the | field shall | clap their | hands.

7 Instead of the thorn shall come up the fir-tree,
And instead of the brier shall come | up the | myrtle-tree:
8 And it shall be to the LORD for a name,
And for an everlasting sign,
That | shall not | be cut | off.

SELECTION 141. [Is. liv. 11–14. & 17.]

1 O thou afflicted, tossed with tempest, | and not | comforted,
2 Behold, I will lay thy stones with fair colors,
And lay thy foundations with sapphires,
And I will make all thy | borders..of | pleasant | stones

3 And all thy children shall be taught of the LORD;
And great shall be the | peace..of thy | children.
4 All thy children shall be taught of the LORD;
And | great shall..be the | peace..of thy | children.

5 In righteousness shalt thou be established:
Thou shalt be far from oppression:
For | thou..shalt not | fear:
6 And from | terror: for it | shall not..come | near thee.

7 No weapon that is formed against thee shall prosper;
And every tongue that shall rise against thee in judg-
ment | thou..shalt con-| demn.
8 This is the heritage of the servants of the LORD;
And their righteousness is of | me,..is of | me..saith the |
LORD.

SELECTION 142. [Is. liv. 7–10.]

1 For a small moment have I forsaken thee;
But with great mercies | will I | gather thee.
2 For a small moment have I forsaken thee;
But with great | mercies..will | I — | gather thee.

3 In a little wrath I hid my face from | thee..for a | moment;
4 But with everlasting kindness will I have mercy on thee,
Saith the | LORD, the | LORD..thy Re-| deemer.

5 For this is as the waters of | Noah..unto | me:
6 For as I have sworn that the waters of Noah, should no more go over the earth;
So have I sworn that I would not be wroth with | thee — | nor re-| buke thee.

7 For the mountains shall depart, and the | hills..be re-| moved;
8 But my kindness shall not depart from thee,
Neither shall the covenant of my peace be removed;
Saith the | LORD..that hath | mercy | on thee.

SELECTION 143. [Is. lvi. 4–7.]

1 Thus saith the LORD unto them that | keep my | Sabbaths;
2 And choose the things that please me,
And take | hold of | my — | covenant;

3 Even unto them will I give in mine house,
And within my walls,
A place and a name better than of | sons..and of | daughters:
4 I will give them an everlasting | name,..that shall | not be..cut | off.

5 Also the sons of the stranger that join themselves to the LORD,
To serve him, and to love the name of the LORD,
To | be his | servants,
6 Every one that keepeth the Sabbath from polluting it,
And taketh | hold of | my — | covenant;

7 Even them will I bring to my holy mountain,
And make them joyful in my | house of | prayer:
8 Their burnt offerings and their sacrifices shall be accepted upon mine altar:
For my house shall be called a house of | prayer for | all — | people.

SELECTION 144. [Is. lviii. 13–14.]

1 If thou turn away thy foot from the Sabbath,
From doing thy pleasure on my | holy | day:
2 And call the Sabbath a delight,
The | holy..of the | LORD — | honorable:

3 And shalt honor him not doing thine own ways,
Nor finding thine own pleasure, nor speaking thine |
own — | words:
4 Then shalt thou de-| light thy-| self..in the | LORD;

5 And I will cause thee to ride upon the high | places..of
the | earth;
6 And feed thee with the heritage of Jacob thy father,
For the | mouth..of the | LORD hath | spoken it.

SELECTION 145. [Is. lxiv. 6–9.]

1 We are all as an unclean thing,
And all our righteousnesses are as | filthy | rags;
2 We all do fade as a leaf;
And our iniquities like the | wind, have | taken..us a-| way:

3 And there is none that calleth upon thy name,
That stirreth up himself to take | hold of | thee:
4 For thou hast hid thy face from us,
And hast consumed us, be-| cause of | our in-| iquities.

5 But now, O LORD, thou art our Father;
We are the clay, and | thou our | potter;
6 And we all are the | work of | thy — | hand.

7 Be not wroth very sore, O LORD,
Neither remember in-| iquity..for-| ever:
8 Behold, see, we beseech thee, | we are | all thy | people.

Is. lxiii. 16.

9 Doubtless thou art our Father,
Though Abraham be ignorant of us, and Israel ac-|
knowledge..us | not:
10 Thou, O LORD, art our Father, and Redeemer;
Thy | name..is from | ever-| lasting.

SELECTION 146. [Is. lxi. 1–3 & 10-11.]

1 The spirit of the LORD GOD, | is up-| on me;

2 Because the LORD hath anointed me to preach good | tidings..un-| to the | meek:

3 He hath sent me to bind up the broken-hearted,
To proclaim liberty to the captives,
And the opening of the prison to | them..that are | bound;

4 To proclaim the acceptable year of the LORD,
And the day of vengeance of our God;
To | comfort | all that | mourn.

5 To appoint unto them that mourn in Zion,
To give unto them | beauty..for | ashes,

6 The oil of joy for mourning,
The garment of | praise..for the | spirit..of | heaviness;

7 That they might be called | Trees of | Righteousness,

8 The planting of the | LORD, that | he..might be | glorified.

9 I will greatly rejoice in the LORD,
My soul shall be | joyful..in my | God:

10 For he hath clothed me with the garments of salvation,
He hath covered me with the | robe, the | robe of | righteousness;

11 For as the earth bringeth forth her bud,
And as the garden causeth the things that are sown in it to | spring — | forth;

12 So the LORD GOD will cause righteousness
And praise to spring | forth be-| fore all | nations.

SELECTION 147. [Mark xi. 9-10.]

1 Hosanna; Blessed is he that cometh in the | name..of the | LORD:

2 Blessed is he that | cometh..in the | name..of the | LORD

3 Blessed be the kingdom of our father David,
That cometh in the | name..of the | LORD:

4 Hosanna, Ho-| sanna, Ho-| sanna..in the | highest.

1 For Zion's sake will I not hold my peace,
And for Jerusalem's sake I | will not | rest;
2 Until the righteousness thereof go forth as brightness,
And the salvation thereof as a | lamp, a | lamp that | burneth.

3 And the Gentiles shall see thy righteousness,
And all | kings thy | glory:
4 And thou shalt be called by a new name,
Which the | mouth..of the | LORD shall | name.

5 Thou shalt also be a crown of glory in the hand of the LORD,
And a royal diadem in the | hand of thy | God.
6 Thou shalt no more be termed forsaken:
Neither shall thy | land be | any..more | Desolate.

7 Thy sun shall no more go down;
Neither shall thy | moon with-| draw itself:
8 For the LORD shall be thine everlasting light,
And the days of thy | mourning | shall be | ended.

9 A little one shall become a thousand,
And a small one a | strong — | nation:
10 I the | LORD will | hasten it..in his | time.

SELECTION 149. [Is. lxii. 6–7. 10–12.]

1 I have set watchmen upon thy walls, O Jerusalem,
Which shall never hold their peace | day nor | night;
2 Ye that make mention of the LORD, keep not silence;
And give him no rest, till he establish,
And till he make Jerusalem a | praise in | all the | earth.

3 Go through, go through the gates;
Prepare you the | way..of the | people;
4 Cast up, cast up the highway;
Gather out the stones; lift up a | standard,..a | standard..for the | people.

5 Behold the LORD hath proclaimed unto the end of the world,
Say ye to the daughter of Zion, Behold, | thy sal..vation | cometh;
6 Behold, his reward is with him,
And his | work, his | work be-| fore him.

7 And they shall call them, The holy people,
The re | deemed..of the | LORD:
8 And thou shalt be called,
Sought | out, A | city..not for-| saken.

SELECTION 150. [Is. lxvi. 1–2.]

1 { Thus saith the LORD, the heaven is my throne,
And the | earth..is my | footstool:

2 { Where is the house that ye build unto me?
And | where..is the | place..of my | rest?

3 { For all those things hath my hand made,
And all those things | have been,..saith the | LORD:

4 { But to this man will I look,
Even to him that is poor and of a contrite spirit,
And | trembleth | at my | word.

Is. lvii. 15.

5 { For thus saith the high and lofty one that in-| habiteth..
e-| ternity,

6 Whose | name, whose | name is | Holy;

7 { I dwell in the high and holy place,
With him also that is of a contrite and | humble | spirit,

8 { To revive the spirit of the humble,
And to revive the | heart..of the | contrite | ones.

SELECTION 151. [Jer. xxxi. 31, 33 & 34.]

1 { Behold, the days come, saith the LORD,
That I will make a new covenant with the house of Israel,
and with the | house of | Judah.

2 { I will put my law in their inward parts,
And write it in their hearts;
And I will be their God, and | they shall | be my | people.

3 { And they shall teach no more every man his neighbor,
And every man his brother, saying, | Know the | LORD;

4 { For they shall know me, from the least of them unto the |
greatest..of | them..saith the | LORD.

5 { For I will forgive their iniquity, and I will remember
their | sin no | more.

6 { I will forgive their iniquity, and will re-| member..their |
sin no | more.

SELECTION 152. [From Zech. 9.]

1 { Rejoice, greatly, O daughter of Zion;
  Shout, O | daughter..of Je-| rusalem:
2 { Behold thy King cometh unto thee;
  He is | just, and | having..sal-| vation.

3 { He shall speak peace unto the heathen;
  And his dominion shall be from | sea to | sea;
4 And from the | river..to the | ends..of the | earth.

5 Turn ye to the strong hold, ye | prisoners..of | hope;
6 Turn ye to the strong | hold, ye | prisoners..of | hope.

SELECTION 153. [Nahum i. 2–7.]

1 { God is jealous, and the LORD revengeth;
  The LORD re-| vengeth,..and is | furious:
2 { The LORD will take vengeance on his adversaries,
  He reserveth | wrath for | his — | enemies.

3 The LORD is slow to anger, and | great in | power;
4 And will not at | all ac-| quit the | wicked.

5 { The LORD hath his way in the | whirlwind..and in th' | storm,
6 And the | clouds..are the | dust..of his | feet.

7 { He rebuketh the sea, and maketh it dry,
  And drieth up | all the | rivers:
8 { Bashan languisheth, and Carmel,
  And the | flower..of | Leba-non | languisheth.

9 { The mountains quake at him, and the hills melt,
  And the earth is | burnt..at his | presence;
10 Yea, the world, and | all that | dwell there-| in.

11 { Who can stand before his indignation?
  And who can abide the | fierceness..of his | anger?
12 { His fury is poured out like fire,
  And the | rocks are..thrown | down by | him.

13 { The LORD is a good, a strong hold in the | day of | trouble:
14 And he | knoweth..them that | trust in | him.

SELECTION 154. [Hosea vi. 1–3.]

1 Come, and let us return unto the Lord:
For he hath torn, and | he will | heal us;
2 He hath smitten, and | he will | bind us | up.

3 After two days will | he re-| vive us:
4 In the third day will he raise us up,
And we shall | live in | his — | sight.

5 Then shall we know,
If we follow on to | know the | Lord:
6 His going forth is prepared as the morning;
And he will come unto us as the rain:
As the latter and former | rain, un-| to the | earth.

SELECTION 155. [Micah iv. 1–4.]

1 But in the last days it shall come to pass,
That the mountain of the house of the Lord
Shall be established in the | top..of the | mountains;
2 And it shall be ex-| alted..a-| bove the | hills:

3 And many nations shall come and say
Come, and let us go up to the | mountain..of the | Lord,
4 And to the | house..of the | God of | Jacob;

5 And he will teach us of..his ways,
And we will | walk..in his | paths.
6 And he will teach us of his ways,
And | we will | walk..in his | paths.

7 For the law shall go forth of Zion,
And the word of the | Lord..from Je-| rusalem.
8 And he shall judge among many people,
And rebuke strong | na..tions a-| far — | off.

9 And they shall beat their swords into plough-shares,
And their | spears..into | pruning-hooks;
10 Nation shall not lift up sword against nation,
Neither | shall they..learn | war..any | more.

11 But every man shall sit under his vine,
And under his fig-tree;
And none shall | make..them a-| fraid;
12 For the mouth of the | Lord of | hosts hath | spoken it.

SELECTION **156.** [Micah vi. 6–8.]

1 { Wherewith shall I come before the LORD,
And bow myself before the | high — | God?
2 { Shall I come before him with burnt offerings,
With | calves..of a | year — | old.

3 { Will the LORD be pleased with thousands of rams,
Or with ten thousands of | rivers..of | oil?
4 { Shall I give my first born for my transgression,
The fruit of my | body..for the | sin..of my | soul?

5 He hath showed thee, O man, | what is | good?
6 { And what doth the LORD require of thee,
But to do justly, and to love mercy,
And to walk | humbly | with thy | God?

SELECTION **157.** [Mal. iii. 1–3.]

1 { Behold, I will send my messenger,
And he shall prepare the | way be-| fore me:
2 { And the LORD whom ye seek,
Shall | suddenly..come | to his | temple.

3 { Even the messenger of the covenant,
Whom | ye de-| light in.
4 { Behold, he shall come,—
He shall | come..saith the | LORD of | hosts.

5 { But who may abide the day of his coming?
And who shall stand when | he ap-| peareth?
6 For he is like a refiner's | fire, and | like..fuller's | soap.

7 And he shall sit as a refiner, and | purifier..of | silver;
8 { And he shall purify the sons of Levi,
And purge them as gold and silver,
That they may offer unto the | LORD an | offering..in |
righteousness.

9 { Then shall the offerings of Judah and Jerusalem
Be pleasant unto the LORD,
As in the days of old as in | former | years.
10 { Then shall the offerings of Judah and Jerusalem
Be pleasant unto the LORD,
As in the days of | old,..as in | former | years.

SELECTION 158. [Deut. xxxii. 1-4.]

1 Give ear, O ye heavens, and | I will | speak;
2 And hear, O | earth, the | words..of my | mouth.

3 { My doctrine shall drop as the rain,
My speech shall dis-| til..as the | dew.
4 { As the small rain upon the tender herb,
And as | showers..up-| on the | grass.

5 Because I will publish the | name..of the | LORD:
6 Ascribe ye | greatness | unto..our | God.

7 { He is Rock, his work is perfect;
For all his | ways are | judgment;
8 { A God of truth and without iniquity,
| Just and | right is | he.

SELECTION 159. [I. Chron. xxix. 10-13]

1 { Blessed be thou, LORD God of Israel our Father,
For | ever..and | ever.
2 { Blessed be thou, LORD God of Israel, our | Father..
For | ever..and | ever.

3 { Thine, O LORD, is the greatness, and the power,
And the glory, and the | victory,..and the | majesty:
4 { For all that is in the | heaven,..and in th' | earth is |
thine;

5 { Thine is the kingdom, O LORD,
And thou art exalted as | head a-bove | all.
6 { Thine is the kingdom, O LORD,
And thou art ex-| alted..as | head a-bove | all.

7 { Both riches and honor come of thee,
And thou | reignest..over | all;
8 { And in thy hand it is to make great,
And to give | strength, give | strength..unto | all.

9 { Now therefore, our God, we thank thee,
And praise thy | glorious | name.
10 { We thank thee,—
And | praise thy | glorious | name.

SELECTION 160. [Exodus xv.]

1 I will sing unto the LORD, for he hath | triumphed | gloriously;
2 The horse and his rider hath he | thrown in-| to the | sea

3 The LORD is my strength and song,
And he is become | my sal-| vation:
4 He is my God, and I will prepare him a habitation,
My | Father's..God and | I..will ex-| alt him.

5 The LORD is a man of war; the | LORD..is his | name.
6 Pharaoh's chariots and his host hath he cast into the sea:
His chosen captains also are | drowned..in the |
Red — | Sea.

7 Thy right hand, O LORD, is become | glorious..in | power:
8 Thy right hand, O LORD, hath | dashed in | pieces..the |
enemy.

9 Who is like unto thee, O LORD, among the gods?
Who is like thee, glorious in holiness, fearful in |
praises,..doing | wonders?
0 Thou in mercy hast led forth the people which thou hast
redeemed;
Thou hast guided them by thy strength unto thy | holy |
habi-| tation.

SELECTION 161. [From Ps. cxix. & Is. lvii]

1 Blessed are they that keep the testimonies of the LORD;
And that seek him with the | whole — | heart.
2 They also do no iniquity; they | walk in | his — | ways.

3 The wicked are like the troubled sea
When it cannot rest,
Whose waters cast up | mire and | dirt.
4 There is no | peace..saith my | God..to the | wicked.

5 Great peace have they who love thy law,
And | nothing..shall of-| fend them.
6 But there is no | peace,..saith my | God..to the | wicked

SELECTION 162. [Luke i. 68-75.]

1 Blessed be the LORD GOD of Israel:
For he hath visited and re-| deemed..his | people,
2 And hath raised up an horn of salvation for us,
In the | house..of his | servant | David:

3 As he spake by the mouth of his holy prophets,
Which have been since the | world be-| gan;
4 That we should be saved from our enemies,
And from the | hand of | all that | hate us.

5 To perform the mercy promised to our fathers,
And to remember his | holy | covenant.
6 The oath which he | sware..to our | father | Abraham,

7 That he would grant unto us,
That we, being delivered out of the | hand of..our | enemies,
8 Might serve him without fear,
In holiness and righteousness before him,
| All the | days..of our | life.

SELECTION 163. [From Ps. l.]

1 The mighty God, even the LORD,
Hath spoken, and called the earth
From the rising of the sun unto the going | down there-| of
2 Out of Zion, the perfection of beauty,
| God — | hath — | shined.

3 "Offer unto God thanksgiving;
"And pay your vows unto the | Most — | High:
4 "And call upon me in the day of trouble;
"I will deliver thee, and | thou shalt | glori-fy | me."

5 "Whoso offereth praise | glori-fieth | me:
6 "And to him that ordereth his conversation aright,
"Will I | show the..sal-| vation..of | God."

SELECTION 164. [Ps. cxvii.]

1 O praise the LORD, all ye nations,
Praise him | all ye | people.
2 For his merciful kindness is great toward us;
And the truth of the LORD endureth forever:
| PRAISE — | YE THE | LORD.

CHANT No. 73.

SELECTION 165. [Ps. cxiv]

1 When Israel went out of Egypt,
The house of Jacob from a people of strange | language.

2 Judah was his sanctuary,
And Israel his do-| minion.

3 The sea saw it and fled;
Jordan was driven | back.

4 The mountains skipped like rams,
And the little hills like | lambs.

5 What ailed thee, O thou sea, that thou fleddest?
Thou Jordan, that thou wast driven | back?

6 Ye mountains, that ye skipped like rams,
And ye little hills, like | lambs? (SYM.)

CHANT No. 74.

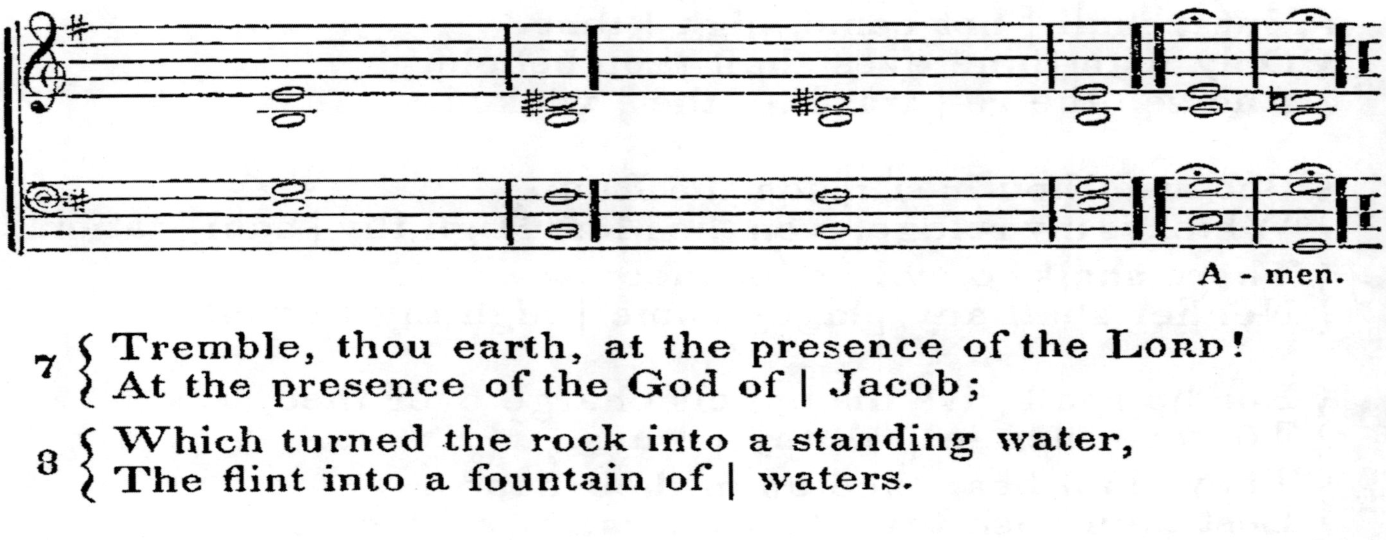

7 Tremble, thou earth, at the presence of the LORD!
At the presence of the God of | Jacob;

8 Which turned the rock into a standing water,
The flint into a fountain of | waters.

CHANT No. 75.

SELECTION 166. [Ps. xci.]

1 He that dwelleth in the secret place of the Most High,
Shall abide under the | shadow..of th'Al-| mighty.

2 I will say of the Lord, He is my refuge, and my fortress:
My God; in | him..will I | trust.

3 Surely he shall deliver thee from the snare of the fowler,
And from the | noisome | pestilence.

4 He shall cover thee with his feathers,
And under his wings shalt thou trust.
His truth shall be thy | shield and | buckler.

5 Thou shalt not be afraid for the terror by night,
Nor for the arrow that | flieth..by | day;

6 Nor for the pestilence that walketh in darkness,
Nor for the destruction that | wasteth..at | noon-day.

7 A thousand shall fall at thy side;
And ten thousand at thy right hand;
But it shall | not come..nigh | thee.

8 Only with thine eyes shalt thou behold,
And see the re-| ward..of the | wicked.

9 Because thou hast made the Lord,
Which is my refuge, even the Most High, thy | habi-| tation.

10 There shall no evil befall thee,
Neither shall any plague come | nigh thy | dwelling.

11 For he shall give his angels charge over thee,
To keep thee in | all thy | ways.

12 They shall bear thee up in their hands,
Lest thou dash thy | foot a-..gainst a | stone.

13 Thou shalt tread upon the lion and adder;
The young lion and the dragon shalt thou | trample.. under | feet.

14 "Because he hath set his love upon me,
"Therefore will I deliver him:
"I will set him on high, because he hath | known my | [name.

15 "He shall call upon me, and I will answer him:
"I will be with him in trouble;
"I will de-| liver him,..and | honor him.

16 With long life will I satisfy him,
And show him | my sal-| vation.

CHANT No. 76.

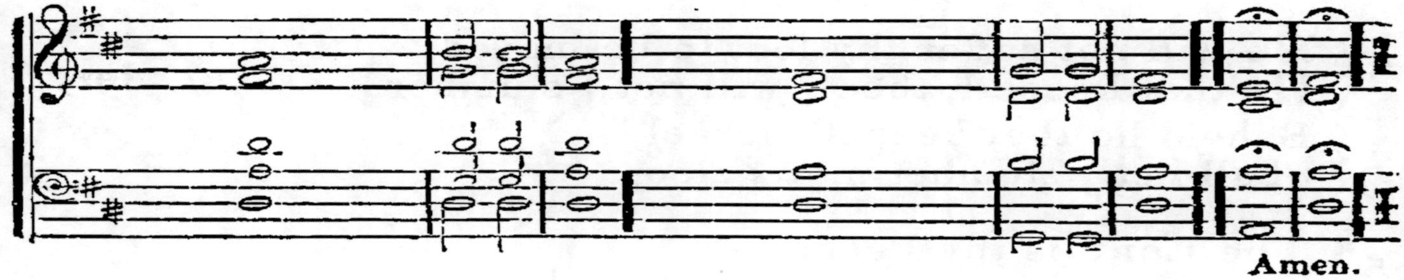

SELECTION 167. [Ps. xxiii.]

1 The Lord is my shepherd; I | shall not | want.

2 He maketh me to lie down in green pastures:
He leadeth me beside the | still — | waters.

3 He restoreth my soul; he leadeth me
In the paths of righteousness for his | name's — | sake,

4 Yea, though I walk through the valley of the shadow of death,
I will fear no evil: for thou art with me;
Thy rod and thy | staff they | comfort me.

5 Thou preparest a table before me
In the presence of mine enemies:
Thou anointest my head with oil;
My | cup..runneth | over.

6 Surely goodness and mercy shall follow me
All the days of my life;
And I shall dwell in the house of the | Lord for-| ever.

CHANT No. 77.

SELECTION 168. [Ps. cxxi.]

1 I will lift up mine eyes unto the hills,
From whence | cometh..my | help.

2 My help cometh from the Lord,
Which made | heaven..and | earth.

3 He will not suffer thy foot to be moved:
He that keepeth thee | will not | slumber.

4 Behold he that keepeth Israel,
Shall not | slumber..nor | sleep.

5 The Lord is thy keeper;
The Lord is thy shade upon thy | right — | hand.

6 The sun shall not smite thee by day,
Nor the | moon by | night.

7 The Lord shall preserve thee from all evil;
He shall pre-| serve thy | soul.

8 The Lord shall preserve thy going out, and thy coming in,
From this time forth, and even for-| ev-er-| more.

SELECTION 169. [Ps. cxii. 1–4.]

1 Blessed is the man that feareth the Lord,
That delighteth greatly in | his com-| mandments.

2 His seed shall be mighty upon earth:
The generation of the upright | shall be | blessed.

3 Wealth and riches shall be in his house.
And his righteousness en-| dureth..for-| ever.

4 Unto the upright there ariseth light in the darkness,
He is gracious, and full of com-| passion..and | righteous.

SELECTION 170. [Ps. cxxv.]

1 They that trust in the Lord shall be as Mount Zion,
Which cannot be removed, but a-| bideth for-| ever.

2 As the mountains are round about Jerusalem,
So the Lord is round about his people,
From | henceforth,..ev'n for-| ever.

3 For the rod of the wicked, shall not rest upon the | lot..
of the | righteous;

4 Lest the righteous put forth their | hands un..to in-| iquity.

5 Do good, O Lord, unto those that are good,
And to them that are | upright..in their | hearts.

6 As for such as turn aside unto their crooked ways.
The Lord shall lead them forth with the workers of iniquity;
But | peace shall..be up-on | Israel.

SELECTION 171. [Ps. xcii. 1–5.]

1 It is a good thing to give thanks unto the Lord,
And to sing praises unto thy name,| O..Most | High:

2 To show forth thy loving-kindness in the morning,
And thy | faithfulness..every | night.

3 Upon an instrument of ten strings, and upon the psaltery;
Upon the harp with a | solemn | sound.

4 For thou, Lord, hast made me glad through thy work;
I will triumph in the | works of..thy | hands.

5 O Lord, how great are thy works,
And thy | thoughts are..very | deep.

6 How great are thy works,——
And thy | thoughts are..very | deep.

CHANT No. 79.

SELECTION 172.

[Ps. cxlviii.]

1 PRAISE YE THE LORD.
Praise ye the LORD from the heavens:
Praise him | in the | heights.

2 Praise ye him, all his angels;
Praise ye him, | all his | hosts.

3 Praise ye him, sun and moon:
Praise him, all ye | stars of | light:

4 Praise him, ye heaven of heavens,
And ye waters that are a-| bove the | heavens.

5 Let them praise the name of the LORD:
For he commanded, and | they..were cre-| ated.

6 He hath also established them forever and ever;
He hath made a decree which | shall not | pass.

7 Praise the Lord from the earth, ye dragons & | all—| deeps:

8 Fire and hail; snow and vapor;
Stormy wind ful-| filling..his | word:

9 Mountains, and all hills; fruitful trees, and | all —| cedars.

10 Beasts, and all cattle; creeping things, and | flying | fowl.

11 Kings of the earth, and all people;
Princes, and all | judges..of the | earth;

12 Both young men and maidens;| old..men and | children.

13 Let them praise the name of the LORD,
For his name a-| lone is | excellent;

14 His glory is above the earth, the | earth and | heaven.

15 He also exalteth the horn of his people,
The praise of | all his | saints.

16 Even of the children of Israel, a people near unto him.
| PRAISE..YE THE | LORD.
Slow.

CHANT No. 80.

SELECTION 173. [Matt. xi. 28.]

1 Come unto me all ye that labor and are | heavy | laden,

2 Come unto me all ye that labor and are heavy laden,
And | I will give you | rest.

3 Take my yoke upon you, and learn of me;
For I am meek and | lowly..in | heart:

4 And ye shall find | rest unto your | souls.

5 For my yoke is easy, and my | burden..is | light

6 For my yoke is easy, and my | burden is—| light. (SYM.)

Rev. xxii. 17.

7 And the Spirit and the bride say, Come.
And let him that | heareth..say,| Come.

8 And let him that is athirst, come:
And whosoever will, let him take the
| water of life—| freely.

SELECTION 174. [Ps. cxxxiii.]

1 Behold how good and how pleasant it is,
For brethren to dwell to-| gether..in | unity.

2 It is like the precious ointment upon the head,
That ran down upon the beard, even Aaron's beard;
That went down to the | skirts of his— | garments.

3 As the dew of Hermon, and as the dew
That descended upon the | mountains..of | Zion.

4 For there the Lord commanded the blessing,
Even | life forever-| more.

 CHANT No. 81. CHANT No. 82.

SELECTION 175. [Ps. xix.]

1 The heavens declare the glory of God;
And the firmament showeth his | handy-|work.
2 Day unto day uttereth speech,
And night unto | night..showeth | knowledge.

3 There is no speech nor language
Where their | voice..is not | heard.
4 Their line is gone out through all the earth,
And their words to the | end..of the | world.

5 In them hath he set a tabernacle for the sun,
Which is as a bridegroom coming out of his chamber,
And rejoiceth as a strong man to | run a | race.
6 His going forth is from the end of the heaven,
And his circuit unto the ends of it,
And there is nothing hid from the | heat there-| of. (SYM.)

7 The law of the LORD is perfect,
Con-| verting..the | soul.
8 The testimony of the LORD is sure,
Making | wise the | simple.

9 The statutes of the LORD are right,
Re-| joicing..the | heart.
10 The commandment of the LORD is pure,
En-| lightening..the | eyes.

11 The fear of the LORD is clean,
En-| during..for-| ever.
12 The judgments of the LORD are true,
And | righteous..alto-| gether.

13 More to be desired are they than gold,
Yea, than much fine gold,
Sweeter also than honey and the | honey-| comb.
14 Moreover by them is thy servant warned,
And in keeping of them there is | great re-| ward.

15 Who can understand his errors?
Cleanse thou me from | secret | faults.

16 Keep back thy servant also from presumptuous sins.
Let them not | have do-minion | over me.

17 Then shall I be upright, and I shall be innocent
From the | great trans-| gression.

18 Let the words of my mouth, and the meditation of my heart,
Be acceptable in thy sight, O LORD, my strength and my
Re-| deemer. A-| men.

CHANT No. 83.

SELECTION 176. [Matt. v. 3–12.]

1 Blessed are the poor in spirit:
For theirs is the kingdom of | heaven.

2 Blessed are they that mourn: for they shall be | comforted.

3 Blessed are the meek: for they shall inherit the | earth.

4 Blessed are they which do hunger and thirst after righteous-
ness: for they shall be | filled.

5 Blessed are the merciful: for they shall obtain | mercy.

6 Blessed are the pure in heart: for they shall see | God.

7 Blessed are the peace-makers:
For they shall be called the children of | God.

8 Blessed are they who are persecuted for righteousness'
sake:
For theirs is the kingdom of | heaven.

9 Blessed are ye when men shall revile you, and persecute
you, and shall say all manner of evil against you falsely,
For | my sake.

10 Rejoice, and be exceeding glad; for great is your reward
in heaven;
For so persecuted they the prophets which were be-| fore you.

CHANT No. 84.

SELECTION 177. [Ps. cxxxvi.]

1 *Verse.* O give thanks unto the Lord, for he is good;
Cho. For his mercy endureth for-| ever.

2 *Verse.* O give thanks unto the God of gods:
Cho. For his mercy endureth for-| ever.

3 *Verse.* O give thanks unto the Lord of lords:
Cho. For his mercy endureth for-| ever.

4 *Verse.* To him who alone doeth great wonders:
Cho. For his mercy endureth for-| ever.

5 *Verse.* To him that by wisdom made the heavens:
Cho. For his mercy endureth for-| ever.

6 *Verse.* To him that stretched out the earth above the waters:
Cho. For his mercy endureth for-| ever.

7 *Verse.* To him that made great lights;
Cho. For his mercy endureth for-| ever.

8 *Verse.* The sun to rule by day: the moon and stars to rule by night:
Cho. For his mercy endureth for-| ever.

9 *Verse.* To him that smote Egypt in their first-born:
Cho. For his mercy endureth for-| ever.

10 *Verse.* And brought out Israel from among them:
Cho. For his mercy endureth for-| ever.

---

11 *Verse.* With a strong hand, and with an out-stretched arm:
Cho. For his mercy endureth for-| ever.

12 *Verse.* To him who divided the Red sea into parts:
Cho. For his mercy endureth for-| ever.

13 *Verse.* And made Israel to pass through the midst of it:
Cho. For his mercy endureth for-| ever.

14 *Verse.* But overthrew Pharaoh and his host in the Red sea:
Cho. For his mercy endureth for-| ever.

15 *Verse.* To him who led his people through the wilderness:
Cho. For his mercy endureth for-| ever.

16 *Verse.* To him who smote great kings: and gave their land for an heritage; even an heritage to Israel his servant:
Cho. For his mercy endureth for-| ever.

---

17 *Verse.* Who remembered us in our low estate:
Cho. For his mercy endureth for-| ever.

18 *Verse.* And hath redeemed us from our enemies:
Cho. For his mercy endureth for-| ever.

19 *Verse.* Who giveth food to all flesh:
Cho. For his mercy endureth for-| ever.

20 *Verse.* O give thanks unto the God of heaven:
Cho. For his mercy endureth for-| ever.

SELECTION 178. [From Ps. cxlvi.]

1 Happy is he that hath the God of Jacob for his help,
Whose hope is in the | Lord his | God.

2 Who made heaven and earth,
The sea, and | all that | therein | is;

3 Which executeth judgment for the oppressed;
Which giveth | food..to the | hungry.

4 The Lord looseth the prisoners;
The Lord | openeth..the | eyes..of the | blind;

5 The Lord raiseth up them that are bowed down;
The Lord | loveth..the | righteous;

6 The Lord preserveth the strangers.
He relieveth the | father-| less and | widow.

7 The Lord shall reign forever;
Even thy God, O Zion, unto | all..gene-| rations.

8 The Lord shall reign forever;
Even thy God, O | Zion,..unto | all..gene-| rations.

SELECTION 179. [Isa. lii. 7-10.]

ORDINATION.

1 How beautiful upon the mountains
Are the feet of him that bringeth good tidings, that | publish-eth | peace;
2 That bringeth good tidings of good, that publisheth salvation;
That saith unto Zion, | Thy —— | God —— | reigneth.

3 Thy watchmen shall lift up the voice;
With the voice together | shall they | sing:
4 For they shall see eye to eye,
When the | Lord shall | bring a..gain | Zion.

5 Break forth into joy, sing together,
Ye waste | places..of Je-| rusalem!
6 For the Lord hath comforted his people,
| He..hath re-| deemed..Je-| rusalem!

7 The Lord hath made bare his holy arm
In the eyes of | all the | nations;
8 And all the ends of the earth
Shall see the sal-| va-tion | of our | God.

SELECTION 180. [Jer. iii. 15.]

ORDINATION.

1 I will give you pastors according to | mine own | heart;
2 That shall feed you with | knowledge..and | under-| standing.

Is. lviii. 1.

3 Cry aloud, spare not, lift up thy | voice..like a | trumpet;
4 Show my people their transgression, and the | house of | Jacob..their | sin.

Is. iii. 10, 11.

5 Say ye to the righteous, that it shall be well with him;
For they shall eat the | fruit..of their | doings.
6 Wo unto the wicked! it shall be ill with him;
For the re-| ward..of his | hands..shall be | given him.

(SYM.)

Acts iv. 29.

7 And now, Lord, grant unto thy servants,
That with all boldness they may | preach thy | word.
8 Grant unto thy servants,
That with all | boldness..they may | preach thy | word.

SELECTION 181. [From Ps. cxxxii.]

DEDICATION.

1 Arise, O LORD, into thy rest;
Thou and the | ark of..thy | strength.
2 Let thy priests be clothed with righteousness;
And let thy | saints — | shout for | joy.
3 The LORD hath chosen Zion:
He hath desired it for | his..habi-| tation.
4 "This is my rest forever:
| Here..will I | dwell..saith the | LORD.
5 "I will abundantly bless her provision;
"I will satisfy her | poor with | bread.
6 "I will also clothe her priests with salvation;
"And her saints shall | shout a-| loud for | joy."

SELECTION 182. [Ps lxxxv. 1–3.]

1 LORD, thou hast been favorable unto thy land:
Thou hast brought back the cap-| tivity..of | Jacob.
2 Thou hast forgiven the iniquity of thy people,
Thou hast | cover-ed | all their | sin.
3 Thou hast taken away all thy wrath;
Thou hast turned thyself from the | fierceness..of thine | anger.
4 Show us thy mercy, O LORD,
And | grant us | thy sal-| vation.

SELECTION 183. [Joel ii. 15-18. 32.]

FAST DAY.

1 Blow the trumpet in Zion,
Sanctify a fast, call a | solemn..as-| sembly:
2 Gather the people, | sancti..fy the | congre-| gation.
3 Let the priests, the ministers of the LORD,
Weep between the | porch..and the | altar,
4 And let them say, Spare thy people O LORD,
And give not thy | heri..tage | to re-| proach.
5 Then will the LORD be jealous for his land,
And | pity..his | people.
6 Yea, the LORD will answer, and it shall come to pass
That whosoever shall call on the name of the | LORD shall | be de-| livered.
7 For in Mount Zion and in Jerusalem shall be deliverance,
As the | LORD hath | said;
8 In Mount Zion and in Jerusalem shall be de-| liverance..
As the | LORD hath | said.

SELECTION 184. [From Daniel ix.]

FAST DAY.

1 O LORD, the great and | dreadful | God,
2 Keeping the covenant and mercy to them that love him,
And to | them that | keep..his com-| mandments.

3 We have sinned, and have com-mitted in-iquity,
And have done wickedly, and | have re-| belled,
4 Even by departing from thy | precepts..and | from thy |
judgments.

5 O LORD, righteousness be-| longeth..unto | thee;
6 But unto us confusion of face, as at this day,
Because we have | sinned..a-| gainst — | thee.

7 To the LORD our God belong mercies and forgivenesses,
Though we have re-| belled a-| gainst him:
8 Neither have we obeyed the voice of the LORD our God,
To walk in his laws, which | he has | set be-| fore us.

9 Now therefore, O our God, hear the prayer of thy ser-
vants, and their | suppli-| cations,
10 And cause thy face to shine upon thy sanctuary that is
| desolate,..for the | LORD'S — | sake.

11 O our God, incline thine | ear and | hear,
12 Open thine eyes, and behold our desolations,
And the city which is | called..by | thy — | name;

13 For we do not present our supplications before thee |
for our | righteousness,
14 But | for thy | great — | mercies.

15 O LORD, hear; O LORD, forgive; O LORD, | hearken,..
and | do;
16 Defer not, for thine own sake, O our God;
For thy city and thy people are | called..by | thy — | name.

SELECTION 185. [Ps. cxi. 9, 10.]

1 The LORD hath sent redemption unto his people:
He hath commanded his | covenant..for-| ever.
2 Holy and | reverend | is his | name.

3 The fear of the LORD, is the be-| ginning..of | wisdom:
4 A good understanding have all | they that | do..his com-|
mandments:

5 His praise en-| dureth..for | ever—
6 His | praise..en-| dureth..for-| ever.

DEDICATION, OR ORDINATION—CLOSE OF SERVICE.

1 Blessed be the LORD, that hath given rest unto his people,
According to | all..that he | promised:
2 There hath not failed one word of all his good promise,
Which he promised by the | hand of | Moses..his | servant.

3 The LORD our God be with us, as he | was..with our | fathers:
4 Let him not | leave us, | nor for-| sake us.

5 That he may incline our | hearts..unto | him;
6 To walk in his ways, and to keep his commandments,
And his statutes, and his judgments,
Which | he..com-| manded..our | fathers.

7 And let the words wherewith we have made supplication
Before the LORD, be nigh unto the LORD our God, | day and | night,..
8 That he may maintain the cause of his servants,
And the cause of his people | Israel..at | all — | times.

9 That all the people of the earth may know that the LORD is God,
And there is | none — | else.
10 Let our heart, therefore, be perfect with the LORD our God,
To walk in his statutes, and to keep his com-| mandments | as at..this | day.

SELECTION 187. [From Ps. lxviii.]

ORDINATION.

1 The LORD gave the word;
Great was the company of | those that | published it.
2 The LORD gave the word;
Great was the | company..of | those that | published it.

3 Thou hast ascended on high,
Thou hast led cap-| tivi..ty | captive;
4 Thou hast received gifts for men,
Yea, for the rebellious also,
That the LORD | God might | dwell a-| mong them.

5 Hallelujah! | A — | men,
6 Hallelujah! | Amen, | A — | men.

DEDICATION.

1 { LORD GOD of Israel, there is no God like thee,
In heaven above, or on | earth be-| neath;
2 { Who keepest covenant and mercy with thy servants,
That walk be-| fore thee..with | all their | heart.

3 { Who hast kept with thy servant David,
| That..thou didst | promise him:
4 { Thou spakest also with thy mouth,
And hast fulfilled it with thine own | hand..as it | is this | day.

5 But will God indeed | dwell..on the | earth?
6 { Behold, the heaven, and heaven of heavens cannot contain thee,
How much less this | house that | we have | builded!

7 { Yet have thou respect unto the prayer of thy servants,
And to their supplication, O | LORD our | God;
8 { Hearken unto the cry and to the prayer,
Which thy servant prayeth be-| fore thee | this — | day.

9 { That thine eyes may be opened toward this house | night and | day,
10 { Even toward the place of which thou hast said,
| "My name | shall be | there."

11 { Hearken thou to the supplication of thy servants,
And of thy people Israel,
Which they shall | make in..this | place.
12 { Hear thou in heaven thy dwelling place,
And | when thou | hearest, for-| give.

II. Chron. vi. 41.

13 { Now therefore arise, O LORD GOD, into thy resting place,
Thou, and the | ark..of thy | strength;
14 { Let thy priests, O LORD GOD, be clothed with salvation,
And let thy | saints re-| joice in | goodness.

SELECTION 189. [Ps. cxxxiv.]

1 Behold, bless ye the LORD, all ye servants | of the | LORD.
2 { Which by night stand in the | house..in the | house..of the | LORD.

3 Lift up your hands in the sanctuary, and | bless the | LORD.
4 { The LORD, that made heaven and earth,
| Bless thee | out of | Zion.

SELECTION 190. [Ps. xcii. 12–15]

1 The righteous shall | flourish..like the | palm-tree.
2 He shall | grow..like a | cedar..in | Lebanon.

3 Those that he planted in the | house..of the | LORD,
4 Shall | flourish..in the | courts of..our | God.

5 They shall still bring forth fruit, in | old — | age,
6 They | shall be | fat and | flourishing;

7 To show that the | LORD is | upright:
8 { He is my rock, and there is no un-| righteous-| ness in | him.

SELECTION 191. [Ps. cviii. 1–5.]

1 { O GOD, my heart is fixed;
I will sing and give praise, | even..with my | glory.
2 { Awake, psaltery and harp;
I my-| self..will a-| wake — | early.

3 { I will praise thee, O LORD, among the people;
And I will sing praises unto thee a-| mong the | nations.
4 { For thy mercy is great above the heavens,
And thy truth | reacheth..un-| to the | clouds.

5 { Be thou exalted, O God, above the heavens,
And thy glory above | all the | earth:
6 { Be thou exalted, O God, above the heavens,
And thy | glory..a-| bove..all th' | earth.

SELECTION 192. [Ps. cxi. 1-4.]

1 { I will praise the LORD with my whole heart,
In the assembly of the upright, and in the | congre-| gation.
2 { The works of the LORD are great,
Sought out of all | them..that have | pleasure..there-| in.

3 { His work is honorable and glorious;
And his righteousness en-| dureth..for-| ever.
4 { He hath made his wonderful works to be remembered;
The LORD is | gracious..and | full..of com-| passion.

CHANT No. 85.

A

CHANT No. 86.

B

CHANT No. 87.

C

SELECTION 193.

TE DEUM LAUDAMUS.*

A

1 { We praise thee, O God;
{ We acknowledge | thee to..be the | Lord.
2 All the earth doth worship thee, the | Father..ever-| lasting.

B

3 { To thee all angels cry aloud;
{ The heavens, and all the | powers there-| in.
4 To thee, cherubim and seraphim con |tinual-| ly do | cry,—

A

5 Holy, holy, holy | Lord .God of | Sabaoth;
6 Heaven and earth are full of the majesty of | thy — | glory.

B

7 The glorious company of the Apostles | praise—| thee,—
Repeat the first part of the chant for this verse.
7 The goodly fellowship of the Prophets | praise—| thee,—
8 The noble army of | Martyrs | praise—| thee.

B

9 The holy church, throughout all the world doth ac-| knowledge | thee,—

10 The Father, of an infinite majesty;
Thine adorable, true, and only Son;
Also the | Holy | Ghost, the | Comforter.

A

11 Thou art the King of | glory,..O | Christ.

12 Thou art the everlasting | Son..of the | Father.

C

13 When thou tookest upon thee to deliver man,
Thou didst humble thyself to be | born..of a | virgin.

14 When thou hadst overcome the sharpness of death,
Thou didst open the kingdom of |Heaven..to|all be-| lievers.

C

15 Thou sittest at the right hand of God, in the | glory..of the | Father.

16 We believe that thou shalt | come to | be our | Judge.

B

17 We therefore pray thee, help thy servants,
Whom thou hast redeemed with thy | precious | blood.

18 Make them to be numbered with thy | saints,
In | glory..ever-| lasting.

A

19 O Lord, save thy people, and bless thine heritage.
Govern them, and lift them | up for-| ever.

20 Day by day we magnify thee;
And we worship thy name, ever,| world with..out | end.

C

21 Vouchsafe, O Lord, to keep us this | day with..out | sin.

22 O Lord, have mercy upon us, have | mer..cy up-| on—| us.

A

23 O Lord,let thy mercy be upon us; as our | trust..is in | thee.

24 O Lord, in thee have I trusted; let me | never..be con-| founded.

---

* This celebrated hymn is said by some to have been written by St. Ambrose, on the occasion of the baptism of St. Augustin. By others it is ascribed to St. Nicetius, Bishop of Triers, who flourished about A. D. 535, nearly 100 years after the death of St Ambrose. "Whoever was the author of the Te Deum, its excellence," says Wheatly, "is surpassed by no human composition. Indeed the composition alone is human, the materials are of divine original."

CHANT No. 88.

CHANT No. 89.

CHANT No. 90.

SELECTION 194.

GLORIA IN EXCELSIS.*

A 1 { Glory be to God on high,
And on earth peace, good | will to | men.

2 { Glory be to God on high,
And on earth | peace, good | will to | men.

3 { We praise thee, we bless thee, we worship thee,
We glorify thee, we give thanks to thee for | thy great | glory.

4 { O Lord God, heavenly King,
| God the | Father | Al—— | mighty.

B 5 O Lord, the only begotten Son, Jesus | Christ;
6 O Lord God, Lamb of God, Son of the | Father;

C 7 That takest away the sin of the | world,
8 Have mercy upon | us.

9 Thou that takest away the sin of the | world,
10 Have mercy upon | us.

---

* This doxology is sometimes called the "Angelic Hymn," because it begins with the song of the angels at Bethlehem. The latter portion of it is ascribed to Telesphorus, about A. D. 139. "In the eastern church," says Palmer, "this hymn is more than 1500 years old, and the church of England has used it for above 1200 years." It is a part of the communion service.

11 Thou that takest away the sin of the | world,
12 Receive our | prayer.

13 Thou that sittest at the right hand of God the | Father,
14 Have mercy upon | us.

A

15 { For thou only art holy;
Thou only | art the | Lord;

16 { Thou only, O Christ, with the Holy Ghost,
Art most high in the | glory..of | God the | Father.

CHANT No. 90.

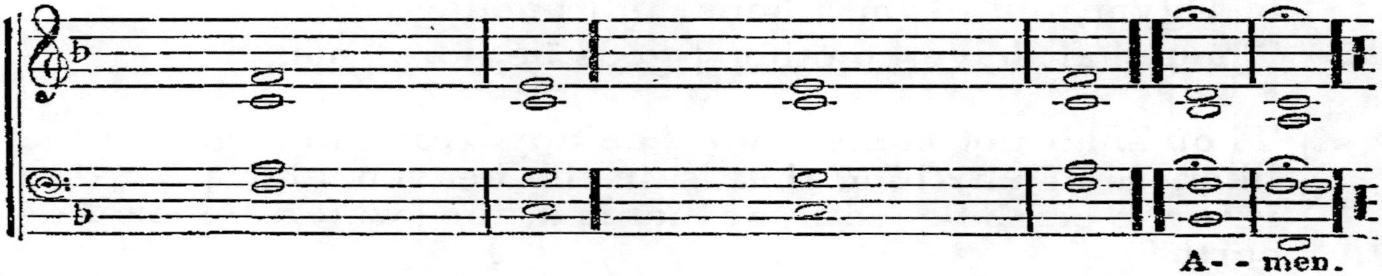

SELECTION 195.

THE LORD'S PRAYER.

1 { Our Father who art in heaven,
Hallowed be thy | name:

2 { Thy kingdom come, thy will be done
On earth, as it is in | heaven.

3 Give us this day our daily | bread;

4 { And forgive us our trespasses,
As we forgive them that trespass against | us.

5 { And lead us not into temptation,
But deliver us from | evil;

6 { For thine is the kingdom, and the power,
And the glory for- | ever.

CHANT No. 91.

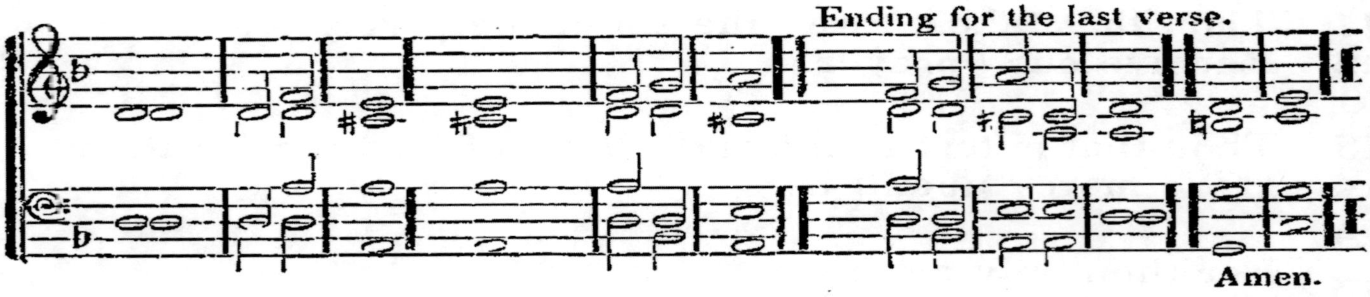

SELECTION 196. [Exod. xx. 1–17.]

THE COMMANDMENTS.

1

1 God spake all these words, saying,—
I am the Lord thy God, which brought thee out of the land of Egypt, out of the | house of | bondage.

2 Thou shalt have no other | gods be..fore | me.

2

3 Thou shalt not make unto thee any graven image, or the likeness of anything that is in the heaven above, or that is in the earth beneath, or that is in the | water..under the | earth:

4 Thou shalt not bow down thyself to them nor serve them; for I the Lord thy God am a jealous God, visiting the iniquity of the fathers upon the children unto the third and fourth generation of them that hate me; and showing mercy unto thousands of them that love me, and | keep..my com-| mandments.

3

5 Thou shalt not take the name of the Lord thy | God in | vain;

6 For the Lord will not hold him guiltless that taketh his | name in | vain.

4

7 Remember the sabbath day, to keep it holy. Six days shalt thou labor, and do all thy work; but the seventh day is the sabbath of the Lord thy God: in it thou shalt not do any work, thou, nor thy son, nor thy daughter, thy man servant, nor thy maid servant, nor thy cattle, nor thy stranger that is with | in thy | gates:

8 For in six days the Lord made the heaven and earth, the sea, and all that in them is, and rested the seventh day: wherefore the Lord blessed the sabbath day, and | hallow-ed | it.

5

9 Honor thy | father..and thy | mother;

10 That thy days may be long upon the land which the
| Lord thy..God | giveth thee.

6

11 Thou shalt not kill.—

7

Thou shalt not commit adultery.—

8

Thou shalt not steal.—

9

Thou shalt not bear false witness a-| gainst thy | neighbor.

10

12 Thou shalt not covet thy neighbor's house, thou shalt not
covet thy neighbor's wife, nor his man-servant, nor his
maid-servant, nor his ox, nor his ass, nor | anything..
that | is thy | neighbor's.

The Metrical Hymns which follow are mostly of an elevated and somewhat peculiar character; but from the irregularity of structure in the different stanzas, or from the great length of the lines, are quite unfit for singing in the common way, that is, to a regular tune or melody. But neither of these circumstances forms the slightest obstacle to chanting; on the contrary, they rather add to the interest of the performance. Thus by the introduction of Chanting, the way is prepared for the use of many hymns, superior in thought and poetic expression, but which on account of a broken rhythm cannot be sung with propriety in the ordinary way, and which have, therefore, been hitherto unavailable in public worship. The chanting of Blank Verse, also, is not only quite practicable, but as the few specimens inserted amongst the following selections will show, it may be made deeply interesting, and highly effective.

CHANT No. 92.

SELECTION 197.

ADORATION.

1

Holy, holy, holy Lord
  God of Hosts! when heaven and earth
Out of darkness, at thy word,
  Issued into | glorious | birth;

All thy works around thee stood,
And thine eye beheld them good,||
While they sang with sweet accord,||
Holy, | holy, | holy | Lord!

2

Holy, holy, holy! Thee,
  One Jehovah evermore,
Father, Son, and Spirit!—We
  Dust and ashes, | would a-| dore.

Lightly by the world esteem'd,
From that world by thee redeem'd,||
Sing we here with glad accord,||
Holy, | holy, | holy | Lord!

3

Holy, holy, holy!—All
  Heaven's triumphant choir shall sing,
While the ransom'd nations fall
  At the | footstool..of their | King:

Then shall saints and seraphim,
Harps and voices, swell one hymn,||
Blending in sublime accord,||
Holy, | holy, | holy | Lord!

Montgomery

SELECTION 198.

ADORATION.

Holy, holy, holy, | Lord..God Al-| mighty!
Early in the morning shall our | song a-| rise to | thee;

Holy, holy, holy! | merci..ful and | mighty!
Je-| hovah! | Father..of e-| ternity!

Holy, holy, holy! | all the..saints a-| dore thee,
Casting down their golden | crowns a-| round the..glassy | sea;

Cherubim and seraphim, falling | down be-| fore thee,
Who wast, and art, and | ever-| more shalt | be!

Holy, holy, holy! | though the..darkness | hide thee,
Though the eye of sinful man thy | glory | may not | see,

Only thou art holy, there is | none be..side | thee,
Perfect in | power,..in | love, and | purity.

Holy, holy, holy, | Lord..God Al-| mighty!
All thy works shall praise thy name, in | earth, and | sky, and | sea.

Holy, holy, holy! | merci..ful and | mighty!
Je-| hovah! | Father..of e-| ternity!

Sale's Coll.

CHANT No. 94.

SELECTION 199.

HUMBLE DEVOTION.

From the recesses of a lowly spirit,
My humble pray'r ascends—O | Father, | hear it!
Borne on the trembling wings of fear and meekness:
For-| give its | weakness.

I know—I feel how mean, and how unworthy
The lowly sacrifice I | pour be | fore thee:
What can I offer thee, O Thou most holy!
But | sin and | folly.

Lord, in thy sight, who ev'ry bosom viewest,
Cold in our warmest vows, and | vain our | truest;
Thoughts of a hurrying hour—our lips repeat them—
Our | hearts for-| get them.
We see thy hand—it leads us—it supports us:
We hear thy voice—it | counsels,..and it | courts us;
And then we turn away! and still thy kindness
For-| gives our | blindness!

Who can resist thy gentle call, appealing
To ev'ry gen'rous thought and | grateful | feeling!
Oh! who can hear the accents of thy mercy,
And | never | love thee.

Kind Benefactor! plant within this bosom
The | seeds of | holiness,|| and let them blossom
In fragrance, and in beauty bright and vernal,
And | spring e-|ternal.

Then place them in those everlasting gardens,
Where angels walk, and | seraphs..are the | wardens;
Where ev'ry flow'r, brought safe through death's dark portal,
Be-| comes im-| mortal.

Bowring.

SELECTION 200.

STAR OF BETHLEHEM.

1

When marshall'd on the nightly plain,
The glittering host be-| stud the | sky,
One star alone, of all the train,
Can fix the | sinner's | wandering | eye.
Hark! hark! to God the chorus breaks,
From every host, from | ev'ry | gem;
But one alone the Savior speaks,—
It is the | Star, the | Star of | Bethlehem!

2

Once on the raging seas I rode;
The storm was loud, the | night was | dark,
The ocean yawn'd, and rudely blow'd
The wind that | toss'd my | foundering | bark
Deep horror then my vitals froze,
Death-struck, I ceas'd the | tide to | stem;
When suddenly a star arose,—
It was the | Star, the | Star of | Bethlehem .

3

It was my guide, my light, my all:
It made my dark fore-| bodings | cease;
And through the storm, and danger's thrall,
It | led me..to the | port of | peace.
Now safely moor'd, my perils o'er,
I'll sing, | first..in night's | diadem,
For ever and for evermore,
The | Star! the | Star of | Bethlehem!

H. K. White.

CHANT No. 96. (Double.)

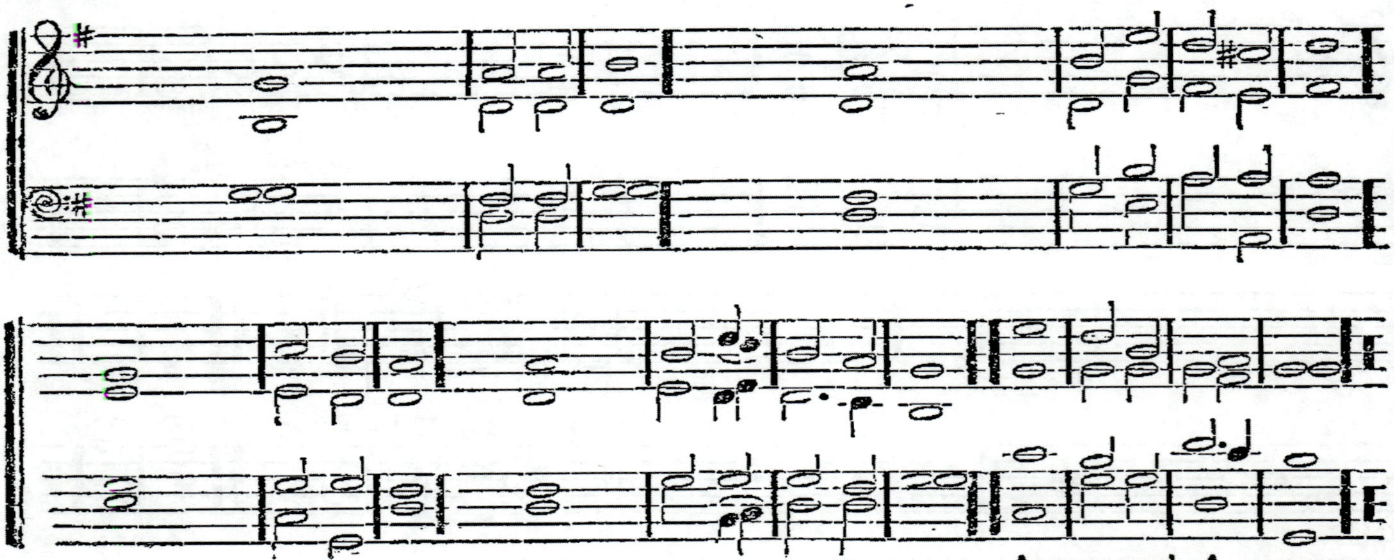

SELECTION 201.

VIEW OF HEAVEN.

1

On wings of faith mount up my soul, and rise,
View thine inheritance be-| yond the | skies.
Nor heart can think, nor mortal tongue can tell,
What endless | pleasures..in those | mansions | dwell.
There our Redeemer lives, all | bright and | glorious,
O'er sin, and death, and | hell, he | reigns vic-| torious.

2

No gnawing grief, no sad heart-rending pain,
In that blest country can ad-| mission | gain;
No sorrow there, no soul-tormenting fear,
For God's own hand shall | wipe the | falling | tear.
There our Redeemer lives, &c.

3

Before the throne a crystal river glides;
Immortal verdure decks its | cheerful | sides;
There the fair tree of life, majestic rears
Its blooming head, and | sov'reign | virtue | bears.
There our Redeemer lives, &c.

4

No rising sun his needless beams displays;
No sickly moon emits her | feeble | rays.
The Godhead there celestial glory sheds:
Th' exalted Lamb e-| ternal | radiance | spreads.
There our Redeemer lives, &c.

5

The distant glimpse my eager passion fires:
To thee, O Lord, my longing | soul as-| pires!
When shall I at thy heavenly home arrive?
When leave this earth, and | when be-| gin to | live?

There is my Savior seen all | bright and | glorious;
O'er sin, and death, and | hell, he | reigns vic-| torious.

Strapham.

CHANT No. 97.

SELECTION 202.

"THY WILL BE DONE."

"Thy will be | done!" || In devious way
The hurrying stream of | life may | run;||
Yet still our grateful hearts shall say,|
"Thy will be | done."

"Thy will be | done!"|| If o'er us shine
A gladd'ning and a | prosp'rous | sun,||
This prayer will make it more divine—|
"Thy will be | done."

"Thy will be done!"|| Though shrouded o'er
Our | path with | gloom,|| one comfort—one
Is ours:—to breathe, while we adore,|
"Thy will be | done."

Bowring

Close by repeating the first two measures—"Thy will be done."

CHANT No. 98.

SELECTION 203.

THE PARDONING GOD.

1

Great God of wonders! all thy ways
  Display thine attributes di-| vine;||
But the fair glories of thy grace,
  Beyond thine other | wonders | shine.
    Who is a pard'ning God like | thee,
    Or who has grace so | rich and | free?

2

Such deep transgressions to forgive,
  Such guilty daring worms to | spare;||
This is thine own prerogative,
  And in the honor | none shall | share.||
    Who is a pard'ning God like | thee,
    Or who has grace so | rich and | free?

3

Pardon—from an offended God!
  Pardon—for sins of deepest | dye!||
Pardon—bestow'd through Jesus' blood!
  Pardon—which brings the | rebel | nigh!||
    Who is a pard'ning God like | thee,
    Or who has grace so | rich and | free? *Davies*

SELECTION 204.

GOD OUR REFUGE.*

1

God is our refuge and defence,
Our shield his | dread Om-| nipotence:‖
Earth may be-| neath us | shrink;
The ancient mountains hoar
Down in the | deep tide | sink;
Let the wild deluge roar!
Jehovah is our | refuge..and de-| fence!

2

There is a river | calm and | pure;
Whose streams refresh and well secure
The | dwelling..place of | God;
Blest city, fair and bright,
His favor'd saints' abode,
Where the | Lord..reigns in | light;
No foe can shake his strong foun-| dations | sure.

3

God is our refuge and our shield,
What then can make us | fear or | yield?
Wars at | his..bidding | cease;
He breaks the bow and spear,
He reigns in | truth and | peace;
Let all adore and fear
Our God and Savior, | Israel's..help and | shield!

* Translated from the German of Luther, being a versification of a part of the 46th psalm; and the same which was set to music, and sung by the great Reformer on the occasion of his journey to Worms, where he was summoned to appear before the Diet, in 1521.

CHANT No. 100. (Double.)

SELECTION 205.

THE HEAD OF SAINTS AND ANGELS.

Hail! great Immanuel, ever honor'd name!
Spread it, ye angels, through heaven's | sacred | frame:
Ye sceptred cherubim before his throne,
And flaming seraphim, | bow — | humbly | down:
He is your Head; with prostrate | awe a-| dore him,
And lay with joy, your | radiant | crowns be-| fore him.

Array'd in his refulgent beams ye shine,
And draw existence from his | source di-| vine;
Grateful, ye wait the signal of his hand,
Pleas'd to obey your | Sov'reign's | high com-| mand;
In Him th' indwelling | Dei..ty ad-| miring,
To bear his brighter | image | still as-| piring.

Mortals with you in cheerful homage join,—
Their sweetest songs of praise with | yours com-| bine:
Mean as we are, with sins and griefs beset,
We glory that in | him we | stand com-| plete:
He is our Head, and we with | you a-| dore him,
And pour our wants, our | joys, our | hearts be-| fore him.

Doddridge.

THE LORD OF GLORY REIGNS.

The Lord of glory reigns supremely great;
High in the heav'ns he builds his | royal | seat;
Through worlds unknown his sov'reign sway extends;
Nor space, nor time his | boundless | empire | ends;
His eye beholds th' affairs of | ev'ry | nation,
And reads each thought through | his im-| mense cre-| ation.

Lightnings and storms his mighty word obey,
And planets roll where he has | mark'd their | way.
Unnumber'd cherubs, veil'd, before him stand,
Waiting the | signal..of his | high com-| mand:
His praise gives harmony to | all their | voices,
And the full choir, in | songs of | praise re-| joices.

Rebellious mortals, cease your tumults vain,
Nor longer such unequal | war main-| tain;
Let clay with fellow-clay in combat strive,
But dread to dare the | Pow'r by | which you | live:
With contrite hearts, fall prostrate, | and a-| dore him,
For if he | frown,..ye | perish,..all, be-| fore him.

Doddridge.

CHANT No. 101. (DOUBLE.)

CHANT No. 102.

SELECTION 207.

CHRIST, AND IMMORTALITY.

1

We sing his love, who once was slain,
  Who soon o'er death re-| viv'd a-| gain,
That all his saints through him might have
  Eternal | conquests | o'er the | grave.
    Soon shall the trumpet sound, and we
    Shall rise to immortality.

2

The saints who now in Jesus sleep,
  His own almighty | power shall | keep,
Till dawns the bright illustrious day,
  When death it-| self shall | die a-| way.
    Soon &c.

3

How loud shall our glad | voices | sing,
  When Christ, his risen saints shall bring
From beds of dust and silent clay,
  To realms of | ever-| lasting | day.
    Soon &c.

4

When Jesus we in glory meet,
  Our utmost joys shall | be com-| plete:
When landed on that heavenly shore,
  Death and the | curse shall | be no | more.
    Soon &c.

R. Hill's Col.

SELECTION 208.

THE COMING OF CHRIST.

1

The chariot! the chariot! its wheels roll in | fire,
As the Lord cometh down in the | pomp..of his | ire;
Self moving it drives on its pathway of | cloud,
And the heavens with the burthen of | God-head are | bow'd.

2

The glory! the glory! around him are | pour'd,
The myriads of angels that | wait..on the | Lord;
And the glorified saints, and the martyrs are | there.
And all who the palm-wreaths of | victo-ry | wear.

3

The trumpet! the trumpet! the dead have all | heard:
Lo, the depths of the stone-cover'd | monuments | stirr'd!
From ocean and earth, from the south pole and | north,
Lo, the vast generation of | ages..come | forth.

4

The judgment, the judgment! the thrones are all | set,
Where the Lamb and the white-vested | elders..are | met;
All flesh is at once in the sight of the | Lord,
And the doom of eternity | hangs..on his | word.

5

O mercy! O mercy! look down from a-| bove,
Redeemer, on us, thy sad | children..with | love!
When beneath to their darkness the wicked are | driven,
May our justified souls find a | wel..come in | heaven!

Rev. H. H. Milman.

CHANT No. 104.

SELECTION 209.

IT IS THE LORD.

1

"It is the Lord!" Behold his hand
Outstretch'd, with an afflictive | rod;
And hark! a voice goes through the land,
"Be still, and know that I am | God!"

2

Shall we, like guilty Adam, hide
In darkest shades our darker | fears?
For who his coming may abide,
Or who shall stand when he ap-| pears?

3

No! let us throng around his seat,
No! let us meet him face to | face—
Prostrate our spirits at his feet,
Confess our sins, and sue for | grace.

4

Who knows but God will hear our cries—
Turn swift destruction from our | path—
Restrain his judgments; or chastise
In tender mercy, not in | wrath;

5

Old Hundred—Key of G. or Chant No. 1.

He will, he will! for Jesus pleads:
Let heaven and earth such love record:
For us, for us, he intercedes:
Our help is nigh—It is the Lord! *Montgomery.*

Amen to be sung after Old Hundred.

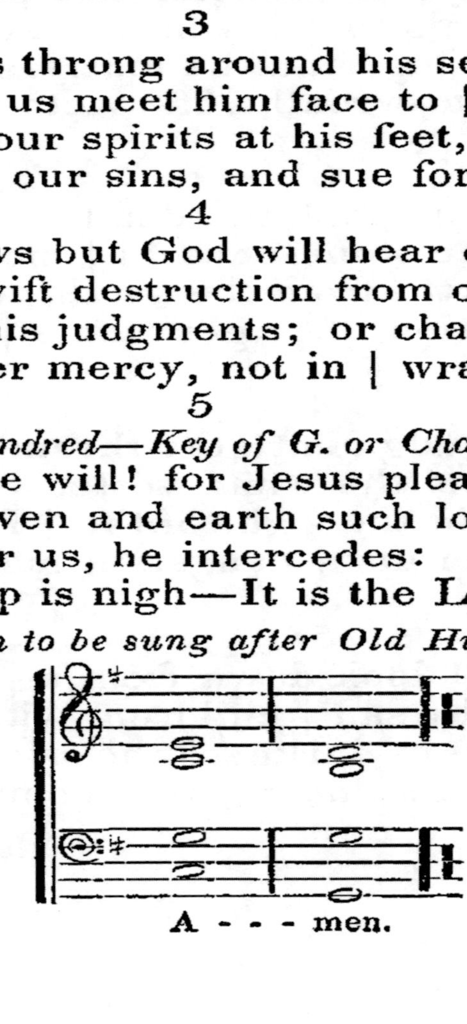

CHANT No. 105.

SELECTION 210.

SEARCHING AFTER GOD.

1

Thou maker of my vital frame,
Unveil thy face, pro-| nounce thy | name;
Shine to my sight, and let the ear
Which thou hast | form'd, thy | language | hear;
  Divide ye clouds, and let me see
  The Power that | gives me | leave to | be.

2

Where is thy residence? Oh! why
Dost thou avoid my | searching | eye;
Mysterious being! Great Unknown,
Say, do the | clouds con-| ceal thy | throne?
  Or art thou all diffus'd abroad,
  Through boundless | space, a | present | God?

3

Is there not some delightful art
To feel thy | presence..at my | heart?
To hear thy whispers, soft and kind,
In | holy | silence..of the | mind?—
  Then rest my thoughts; no longer roam
  In quest of | joy—for | heaven's at | home!

Watts

A

CHANT No. 106.

B

CHANT No. 107.

C

CHANT No. 108.

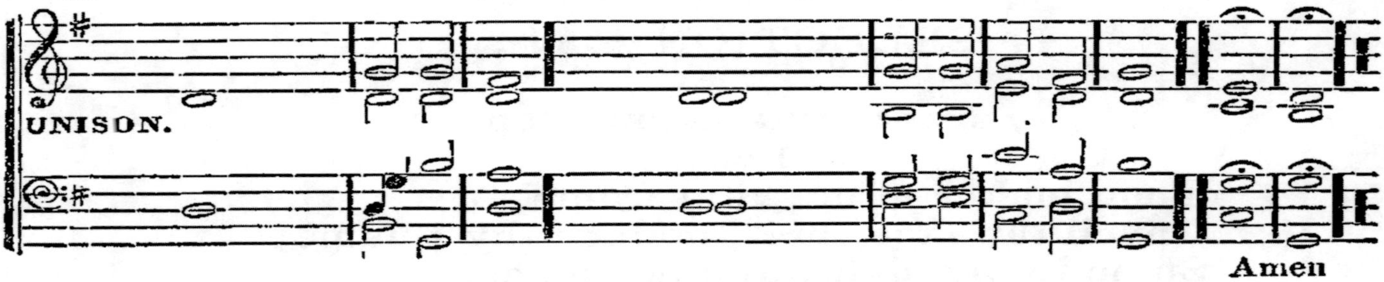

SELECTION 211.

THE LIVING AND THE DEAD.

A

1

Where are the dead? In heaven or hell,
Their disembodied | spirits | dwell;
Their buried forms, in bonds of clay,
Reserved un-| til the | judgment-| day.

2

Who are the dead? The sons of time,
In every age, and | state, and | clime;
Renown'd, dishonor'd—or forgot,
The place that | knew them | knows them | not.

B

3

Where are the living? On the ground,
Where prayer is heard, and | mercy | found;
Where, in the period of a span,
The mortal | makes th' im-| mor-tal | man.

4

Who are the living? They whose breath
Draws every moment | nigh to | death;
Of bliss or woe th' eternal heirs?
Oh! what an | awful | choice is | theirs!

C 5

This Stanza may be sung to Chant C, or to Old Hundred.

Then timely warn'd, may we begin
To follow Christ, and | flee from | sin;
Daily grow up in him our head,
| Lord..of the | living..and the | dead. *Montgomery.*

A **CHANT No. 109.**

B **CHANT No. 110.**

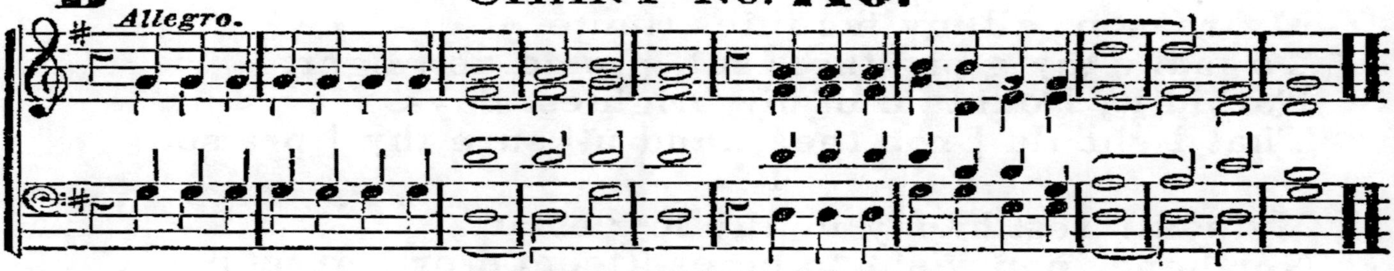

SELECTION 212.

GOD THE UNIVERSAL KING.

1

A Hark the glad shout! our God to conquest leads,
Triumphant sounds proclaim his | glorious | name!
Join every voice in hymns of joyful praise;
Our God, our King, de-| mands the | sacred | song:

B Repeat his praises in immortal strains.

2

A For God is king supreme, o'er all the earth
With uncontested power his | sceptre | rules:
And while his praise employs the tuneful voice,
Let all your hearts a-| dore the | name you | sing.

B Repeat his praises &c.

3

A Sole monarch of the world Je-| hovah | reigns!
The heathen empires trembling own his power,
And holiness sur-| rounds his | awful | throne.

B Repeat his praises &c.

4

A Great | is the | Lord!—his high exalted name
Forever with un-| rivall'd | glory | shines.

B Repeat his praises &c. *From Mrs. Steele.*

SELECTION 213.

The following Hymns may be sung to any appropriate Chant.

GLORY TO GOD ALONE.

1

Oh lov'd! but not enough—though dearer far
Than self, and its most lov'd en-| joyments | are;
None duly loves thee, but who, nobly free
From sensual objects, | finds his | all in | thee.

2

Glorious, Almighty, First, and Without End!
When wilt thou melt the mountains | and de-| scend?
When wilt thou spread abroad thy conquering rays,
And teach these | atoms,..thou hast | made, thy | praise?

3

My reason, all my faculties, unite
To make thy glory their su-| preme de-| light;
Forbid it, Fountain of my brightest days,
That I should | rob thee,..and u-| surp thy | praise.

4

My soul! rest happy in thy low estate,
Nor hope, nor wish, to be es-| teem'd or | great;
To take th' impression of a will divine,
Be that thy glory, and | those — | riches | thine

5

Confess him righteous in his just decrees,
Love what he loves, and let his | pleasure | please;
Die daily; from the touch of sin recede;
Then thou hast | crown'd him,..and he | reigns in-| deed

Guion, translated by Cowper.

SELECTION 214.

GOD ONLY KNOWS HIMSELF.

1

Stand and adore; how glorious He
That dwells in | bright e-| ternity!
We gaze, and we confound our sight,
Plung'd in the a-| byss of | dazzling | light!

2

Seraphs, the nearest to the throne,
Begin, and speak the | Great Un-| known:
Attempt the song, and tune your strings
To notes un-| tried, and | boundless | things!

3

You, whose capacious powers survey
Far, far beyond our | eyes of | clay:
Yet what a narrow portion too
Is seen, or | known, or | thought, by | you!

4

How far your highest praises fall
Below th' im-| mense O-| riginal!
Weak creatures we, that strive in vain
To reach an | uncre-| ated | strain!

5

Great God, forgive our feeble lays;
Sound forth thine own e-| ternal | praise;
A song so vast, a theme so high,
Calls for the | voice that | tun'd the | sky.

Watts.

SELECTION 215.

THE VOICE OF GOD.

1

Oh! blest were the accents of early creation,
When the word of Jehovah came | down..from a-| bove;
In the clods of the earth to infuse animation,
And wake their cold | atoms..to | life..and to | love.

2

And mighty the tones which the firmament rended,
When on wheels of the thunder and | wings..of the | wind,
By lightnings and hail, and thick darkness attended,
He utter'd on | Sinai..his | laws to..man-| kind.

3

And sweet was the voice of the First-born of heaven,
Though poor his apparel, though | earthly.. his | form,
Who said to the mourner, "Thy sins are forgiven!"
'Be whole,' to the | sick,—and 'be | still,' to the | storm.

4

Oh! Judge of the world! when array'd in thy glory,
Thy summons again shall be | heard..from on | high,
While nature stands trembling, and naked before thee,
And waits on thy | sentence..to | live,..or to | die,

5

When the heav'n shall fly fast from the sound of thy thunder,
And the sun in thy lightnings grows | languid..and | pale:
And the sea yield her dead, and the tomb cleave asunder—
In the hour of thy | terrors,..let | mercy pre-| vail.

Bishop Heber.

SELECTION 216.

THE NATIVITY: OR, CHRISTMAS DAY.

1

Ye tempests spare the slumbers of your Lord!
Ye Zephyrs, all your whisper'd | sweets af-| ford!
Confess the God that guides the rolling year;
Heaven, do him homage, and | thou — | earth re-| vere!

2

Ye shepherds, monarchs, sages, hither bring
Your hearts an offering, and a-| dore your | King!
To Bethlehem haste, rejoice in his repose,
And praise him there for | all that | he be-| stows.

3

Perverted reason revels, and runs wild,
By glittering shows of pomp and | wealth be-| guil'd;
And blind to genuine excellence and grace,
Finds not her | author..in so | mean a | place.

4

Ye unbelieving; act a wiser part,
Distrust your erring sense, and | search your | heart:
'Tis there ye shall perceive the kindling flame,
Acknowledging the | God from | whom it | came.

Guion, translated by Cowper.

SELECTION 217.

THE DAY OF JUDGMENT.

1

When the fierce north wind, with his airy forces
Rears up the Baltic to a | foaming | fury;
And the red lightning, with a storm of | hail comes |
Rushing a..main | down,

2

How the poor sailors stand a-| maz'd, and | tremble!
While the hoarse thunder, like a bloody trumpet,
Roars a fierce onset to the gaping waters
| Quick..to de-| vour — | them.

3

Such shall the noise be, and the wild disorder,
(If things eternal may | be like..those | earthly) —
Such the dire terror when the great arch | angel |
Shakes..the cre-| ation;

4

Tears the strong pillars of the vault of heaven,
Breaks up old marble, the re-| pose of | princes:
While the dread summons thunders through death's caverns,
| "Come — | all to | judgment."

5

See the sky parting, and the judge descending!
Now let our praises all a-| rise to | Jesus;
How he sits God-like! and the saints around him
| Thron'd, | yet a-| doring.

6

Oh! may I sit there when he comes triumphant,
| Dooming..the | nations! || then ascend to glory,
While loud hosannas all along the passage
| Shout — | the Re-| deemer.

Watts

SELECTION 218.

PRAISE TO GOD.

1

From vocal air, and concave skies,
Let wafted | halle..lujah's | sound;
And let the sacred triumphs rise,
Till vaulted | heaven the | notes re-| bound.

2

Thou solar orb! whose ruddy beam
Compels the shades of | night to | yield;
Thou silver moon! whose fainter gleam
Scarce | trembles..o'er yon | azure | field!

3

Ye stars! who circle round the pole,
Illumin'd with dis-| tinguish'd | rays:
Instruct your vocal spheres to roll,
Sym-| phonious..to your | Maker's | praise.

4

His name with pious praises sing,
Who kindled first the | beamy | light:
Who first commanded you to spring
Forth from the | cells of | ancient | night.

5

Ye active youths, in manly prime!
Ye virgins deck'd with | blooming | grace.
Ye elders press'd by creeping time!
And | you, ye | tender..infant | race!

6

Your voices raise with mix'd acclaim,
To praise the uni-| versal | Lord;
The sole, august, majestic name,
O'er earth and | heav'n, by | all a-| dor'd.

Mrs. Tollet

SELECTION 219.

GOD THE SPIRIT.

1

O God, thou art a Spirit, pure,
Invisible to | mortal | eyes;
Th' immortal and th' eternal King,
The great, the | good, the | only | wise.

2

While nature changes, and her works
Decay, corrupt, dis-| solve, and | die;
Thy essence pure no change shall see,
Se-| cure of | immor-| tality.

3

Thou great Invisible! what hand
Can draw thy image | spotless | fair;
To what in heav'n, to what on earth,
Can men th' im-| mortal | King com-| pare?

4

Let stupid heathen frame their gods
Of gold, of silver, | wood and | stone;
Ours is the God that made the heavens;
The great Je-| hovah, | God a-| lone.

5

My soul, thy purest homage pay,
In truth, and spirit | him a-| dore:
More shall this please than sacrifice,
Than outward | forms de-| light him | more.

Needham.

SELECTION 220.

VIEW OF CREATION.

Sing to Chant No. 1.

1

Look up, ye saints! direct your eyes
To him who dwells a-| bove the | skies;
With your glad notes his praise rehearse,
Who | form'd the | mighty | universe.

2

He spake, and from chaotic night
At once sprang forth the | cheering | light:
Him discord heard; and, at his rod,
Expanded | beauty | spoke the | God.

3

The word he gave,—th' obedient sun
Began his glorious | race to | run;
Nor silver moon, nor stars delay
To glide a-| long..th' e-| thereal | way.

4

Teeming with life:—air, earth, and sea,
Obey th' Almighty's | high de-| cree;
To every tribe he gives their food,
Then speaks the | whole di-| vinely | good.

5

But, to complete the wondrous plan,
From earth and dust he | fashions | man;
In man the last, in him the best,
The maker's | image | stands con-| fest.

6

Old Hundred Key of G.

Lord, while thy glorious works I view,
Form thou my heart and soul anew;
Here bid thy purest light to shine,
And beauty glow with charms divine.

Needham.

SELECTION 221.

WORLD FORSAKEN.

1

No more vain world, with thy alluring toys,
No more ensnare my easy | yielding | heart:
Vanish, ye unsubstantial airy forms,
Delusive shadows, cheat mine eyes no more
With | painted | shows of | pleasure.

2

One ray of heaven, bright dawning o'er my soul,
Eclipses all your | vision..ary | charms,
And points to | happi..ness be-| yond your | reach.

3 (SYM.)

Ye sons of harmony, who ardent tune
To boundless joy the heaven re-| sounding | song;
Oh! could I hear your rapture breathing strains,
How would my kindling powers awake to praise,
And join with | ecsta-sy the | blissful | theme;

4

Earth's flattering trifles then should | tempt in | vain,
Nor interrupt my | sweet, my | blest em-| ploy.

From Mrs. Steele

SELECTION 222.

SUPPLICATION.

1

O Thou, great source of every good! by whom
This heart was taught to beat, these thoughts to range
O'er the wide | circuit..of the | universe,
To soar beyond the farthest bounds of time,
And pant for bliss, which | earth could | ne'er be-| stow;

2

While worlds, unnumber'd, tremble at thy power,
And hosts, celestial, own their loftiest strain
Too weak to | tell thy | praise—
Oh! how shall | man
E'er | lift his..voice to | Thee?

3

Yet, at thy call,
Thy servant comes; Oh! hear my | humble | prayer:
By thy almighty power direct, sus-| tain
My | feeble | efforts;

4

And whate'er the lot
To me on | earth as-| sign'd,
Oh! guide me still,
By the blest light of thy eternal truth,
Through every varied | scene of | joy or | woe;

5

Support my weakness by thy | mighty | aid,
And lead my soul to | peace, to | bliss, to | Thee!

Bowdler.

SELECTION 223.

FOR DIVINE ILLUMINATION.

1

O Thou, whose power o'er moving worlds presides,
Whose voice created, and whose | wisdom | guides;
On darkling man in pure effulgence shine,
And cheer the clouded | mind with | light di-| vine!

2

'Tis thine alone to calm the pious breast,
With silent confidence and | holy | rest;
From thee, Great God! we spring—to thee we bend,
Path, Motive, | Guide, O-| rigi..nal and | end!

Dr. Johnson.

SELECTION 224.

THE LATTER DAY GLORY.

1

Rise, crown'd with light, imperial Salem, rise!
Exalt thy towery head, and | lift thy | eyes!
See barbarous nations at thy gates attend,
Walk in thy light, and | in thy | temple | bend!

2

No more the rising sun shall gild the morn,
Nor evening moon shall fill her | silver | horn:
But in thy courts, THE LIGHT HIMSELF shall shine
Reveal'd, and God's e-| ternal | day be | thine!

3

The seas shall waste, the skies in smoke decay,
Rocks fall to dust, and mountains | melt a-| way;
But fix'd his word, his saving power remains—
Thy realm for ever | lasts, thy | own Mes-siah | reigns!

Pope.

SELECTION 225.

GOD THE CREATOR ADORED.

1

Almighty former of this wondrous plan,
Faintly reflected in thine | image, | Man—
Holy and just—the greatness of whose name
Fills and sup-| ports this | uni..versal | frame.

2

Diffus'd throughout th' infinitude of space,
Who art thyself thine | own vast | dwelling-place;
Soul of our soul, whom yet no sense of ours
Discerns, e-| luding..our most | active | powers.

3

Encircling shades attend thine awful throne,
That veil thy face, and keep thee | still un-| known;
Unknown, though dwelling in our inmost part,
Lord of our | thoughts, and | sov'reign..of the | heart!

4

All darkness flies when thou art pleas'd t' appear,
A sudden spring renews the | fading | year;
Where'er I turn, I see thy power and grace,
The watchful | guardians..of our | heedless | race.

5

Thy various creatures in one strain agree,
All, in all times and places, | speak of | thee;
Ev'n I, with trembling heart and faltering tongue,
Attempt thy | praise, and | join the..general | song.

Guion, translated by Cowper.

SELECTION 226.

GOD'S PRESENCE DESIRED, AND PRAYER FOR PARDON.

1

Let the world frown, and all its | pleasures | fly,
Let every earthly comfort disappear,
And all the charms of | nature | sink in | darkness!—

2

If thou art with me, if | thou..art my | God,
Am I not | happy?..can I | wish for | more?

3

Thy gracious presence well supplies the loss
Of | earthly | bliss;
and yields superior joy
To all that | uni..versal | nature | boasts!

4

My God! oh! may I call thee | mine in-| deed!
And may the humble breathings of my soul,
Accepted rise be-| fore thy | throne of | grace:

5

In his dear name I come, and | plead his | merits,
Who died, and rose, and intercedes a-| bove
For | guilty | rebels!

6

reconciled in him,
Smile, | on my | soul,
and | save me | from my | sin!

7

Oh! let thy gracious visits cheer my heart
In | this sad | wilderness,—
and light my passage
Through the last gloomy | scene, the | shades of | death!

8

Then raise me to those bright, those blest abodes,
Where thy kind presence with unclouded ray
For-| ever | shines!
full joys forever smile
And pleasure | triumphs..in im-| mortal | bloom.

From Mrs. Steele.

SELECTION 227.

CHOOSING CHRIST.

1

My Lord, my Savior, my Almighty friend,
Oh! wilt thou, gracious, own the | humble | claim!
And let thy Spirit, sacred evidence,
Confirm it to my | soul with | power di-| vine!

2

Tell me, Oh! tell me thou art | mine in-| deed,
And fill my | heart with | grati..tude and | love! (SYM.)

3

But ah! how weak, how languishing, and low,
My strongest gratitude, my | highest | love:
How cold the warmest ardors of my soul
For | blessings | so di-| vine!

4

how poor a gift,
This | wretched..sinful | heart!
and yet 'tis all
A worthless worm can offer,
Nor can I tender | this, with-| out thy | aid;

5

O help me to surrender | all my | heart,
Its powers and | passions..to thy | sovereign | love!

6

Accept it, Lord, and make it | thine en-| tire!
Let thy abounding grace remove my guilt,
Forgive my wanderings, | fix me | thine for-| ever.

Mrs. Steele.

SELECTION 228.

FROM THE 46TH PSALM.

1

There is a river of immortal peace,
Clear springing from the high e-| ternal | throne,
Which flows in blissful streams through | all the | groves
Of | paradise;

2

from this eternal spring
Some little rivulets descend, to cheer
The | city..of our | God,—
the sacred place
Of | his a-| bode on | earth;

3

though all around
Be | discord..and com-| motion,—
she shall dwell
Unmov'd, serene, and | safe, for | God is | there:

4

His arm omnipotent is | ever | near,
Her present | help,..her | all-suf..ficient | guard.

5

The Lord of | hosts is | with us;
Israel's God
Is our defence, our | ever-| lasting | refuge.

Mrs. Steele.

SELECTION 229.

GOD'S WATCHFUL CARE OVER HIS PEOPLE.

1

——With watchful eye, and tender care,
The Lord regards the souls that | fear his | name,
Who on his sovereign | mercy | fix their | hope:

2

He guards their lives from every | deathful | stroke; |
Nor war shall hurt them, | nor shall | famine | waste.

3

On him we wait, our God, our | help, our | shield;
On him with humble | confi-| dence de-| pend.

4

In him our souls forever | shall re-| joice;
For we have | trusted..in his | holy | name.

5

Oh! be thy mercy, Lord, our constant trust,
Our | blissful | portion,—
mercy large and full,
Unbounded and im-| mortal | as our | hopes.

From Mrs. Steele.

SELECTION 230.

PRAYER FOR SUPPORT IN DEATH.

1

Jesus, my Lord, on thee alone my | all de-| pends,
My | ever-| lasting | all!

2

in that dread hour,
When earthly | comforts | fail;
oh! let me feel
Thy love, sweet cordial to my fainting heart!
In-| fusing | strength di-| vine;

3

its vital force
Shall bid me rise superior in the conflict
With | nature's | foe,—
and tune my quivering | lips
To | holy | rapture!

4

let thy glorious name,
My Lord, my Savior, | dwell up..on my | tongue!
Till my glad spirit quits her house of clay,
Ascends to God, and joins the song triumphant,
To | my Re-| deemer's | praise.

From Mrs. Steele.

SELECTION 231.

THE LORD'S PRAYER.

ARRANGED FOR ANY REGULAR CHANT.

1 { Our Father who art in heaven,
Hallowed | be thy | name:
2 { Thy kingdom come; thy will be done
On | earth, as it | is in | heaven.

3 Give us this day our | daily | bread;
4 { And forgive us our debts,
As | we for-| give our | debtors

5 { And lead us not into temptation,
But deliver | us from | evil:
6 { For thine is the kingdom,
And the power, and the | glory,..for-| ever..and | ever.

SELECTION 232.

GLORIA PATRI.

A DOXOLOGY OF THE PRIMITIVE CHURCH.

Glory be to the Father, and to the Son, and to the | Holy | Ghost;
As it was in the beginning, is now, and ever | shall be | world with..out | end.

CHANT No. 111. (MAJOR OR MINOR.)

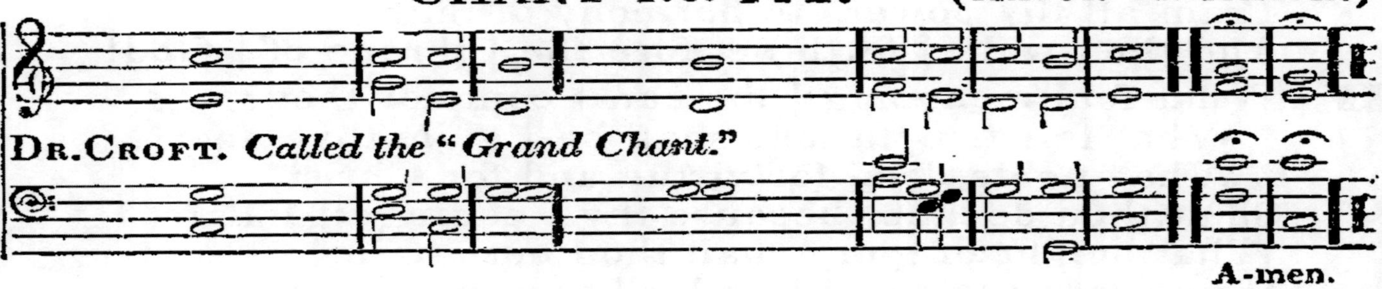

CHANT No. 112.

A CHANT No. 113.

B CHANT No. 114.

C CHANT No. 115.

SELECTION 233.

THE CHRISTIAN URGED ONWARD, AND ENCOURAGED TO RELY ON THE WORD OF GOD.

A Gird on thy armor, warrior of the Lord;
Bind to thy heart God's | ever..lasting | truth;
Train all thy powers to harmony of faith,
And then walk | forth be..fore the | throne of | God!

B What foul menacing | foe can | conquer thee?
* What fair temptations shall be-| guile thy | feet?
* What noble deed for virtue and for Christ,
Shalt thou decline, because thy | courage | fails?
What height of glory shall thou not attain,
If upward still, thy | Leader | thou pur-| sue?

C All heaven doth beckon thee! arise! ascend!

A Fear not! | oh,— | faint not!
Lo, the word of God,
Forever sure—eternally the same,
Boundless in its relations – in its scope
Sublime —transcendent in its loveliness,
And in its holy grandeur overwhelming —
Is round a-| bout thee..and is | thine for-| ever.

Rev. N. E. Johnson.

* Repeat the first strain of the Music.

CHANT No. 116.

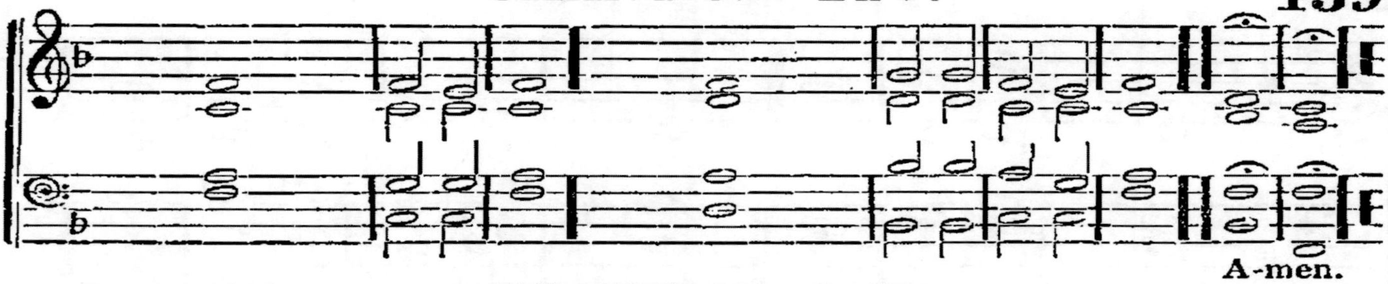

CHANT No. 117.

CHANT No. 118.

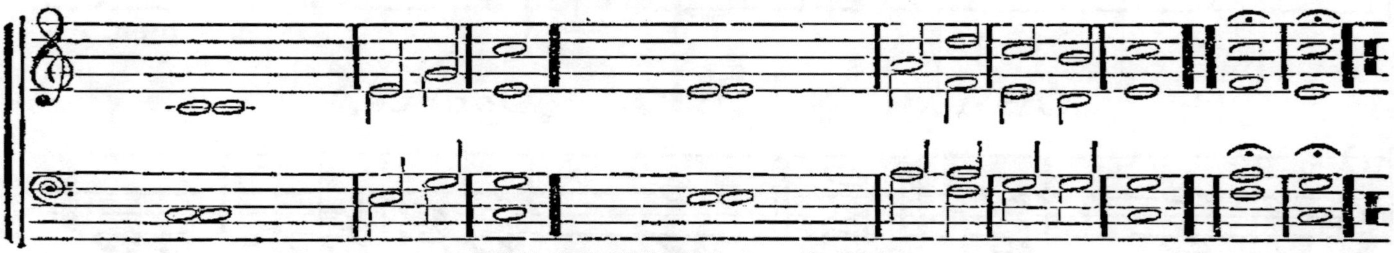

CHANT No. 119.

CHANT No. 120.

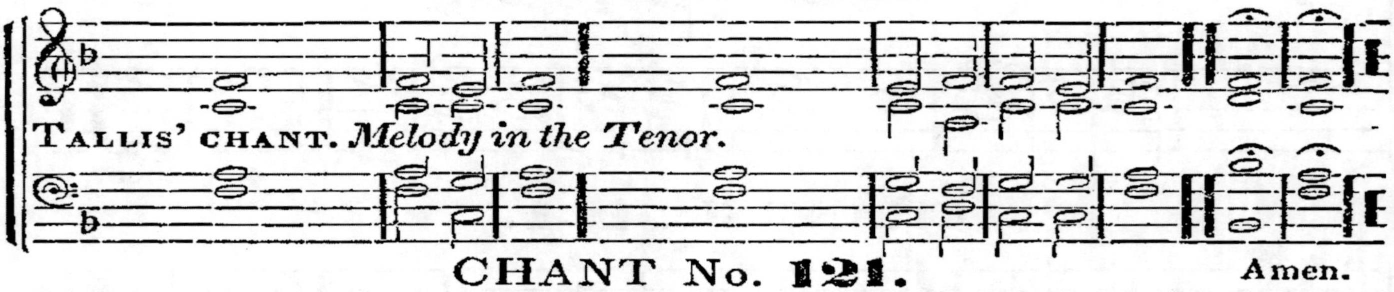

CHANT No. 121.

CHANT No. 122. (Double.)

CHANT No. 123. (Double.)

CHANT No. 124.

CHANT No. 125. (Double.)

CHANT No. 126. (Double.)

CHANT No. 127.

14*

CHANT No. 128. (Double.)

CHANT No. 129. (Double.)

CHANT No. 130.

CHANT No. 131.

CHANT No. 132.

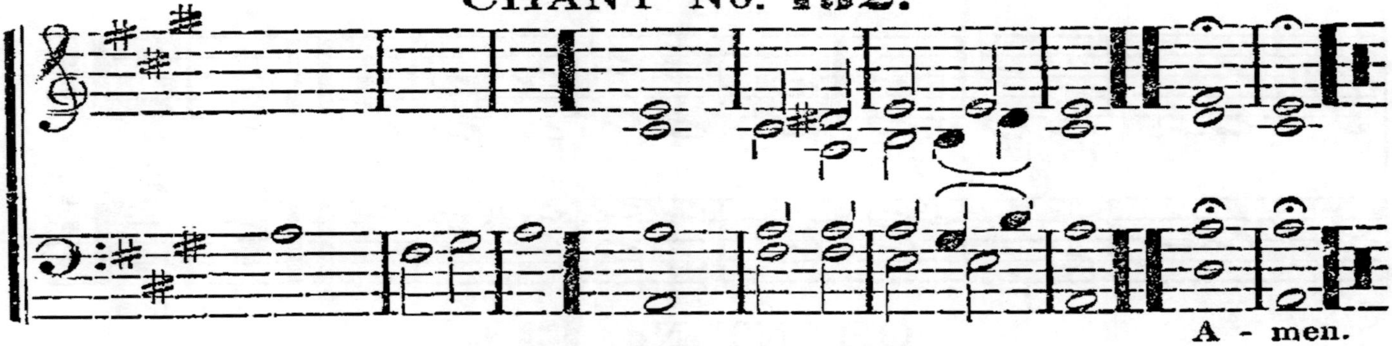

CHANT. No. 133.

CHANT. No. 134.

CHÀNT No. 135.

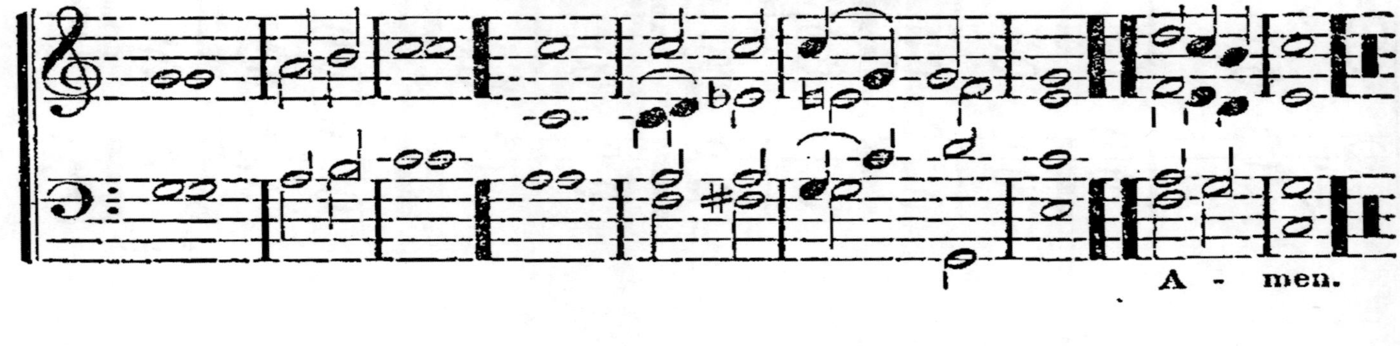

CHANT No. 136.

CHANT No. 137.

CHANT No. 138.

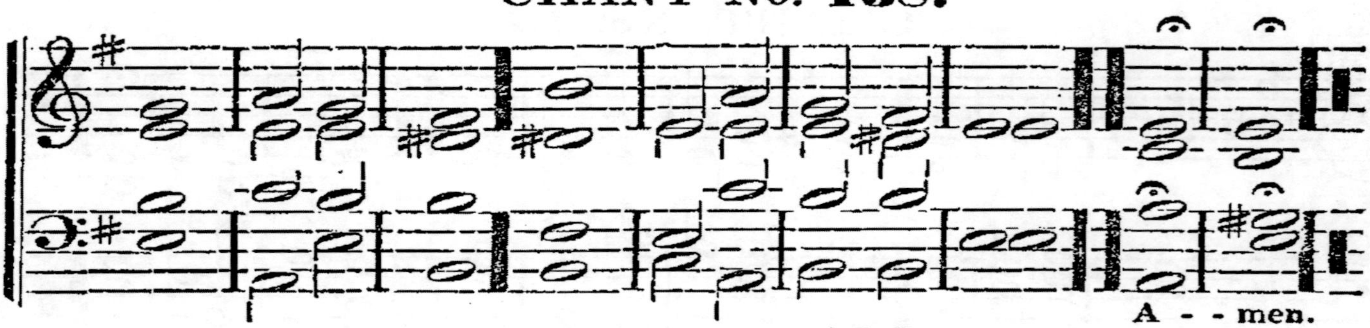

CHANT No. 139.

CHANT No. 140.

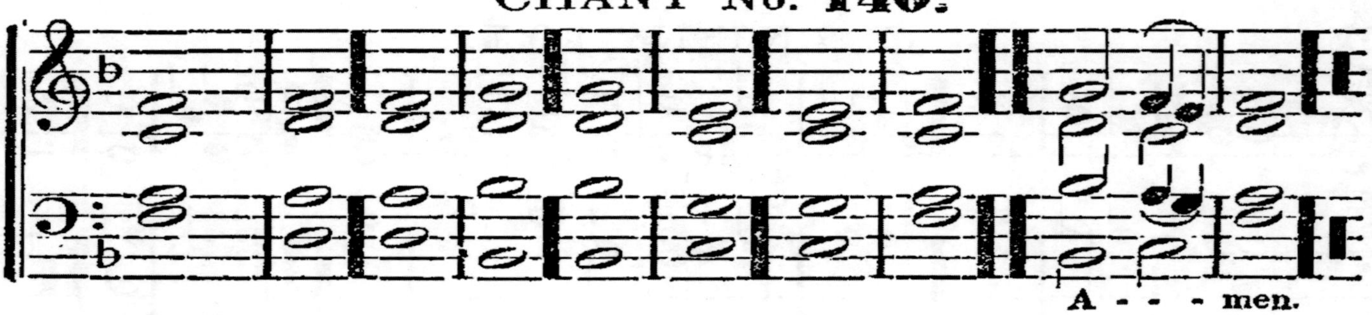

CHANT. No. 141.

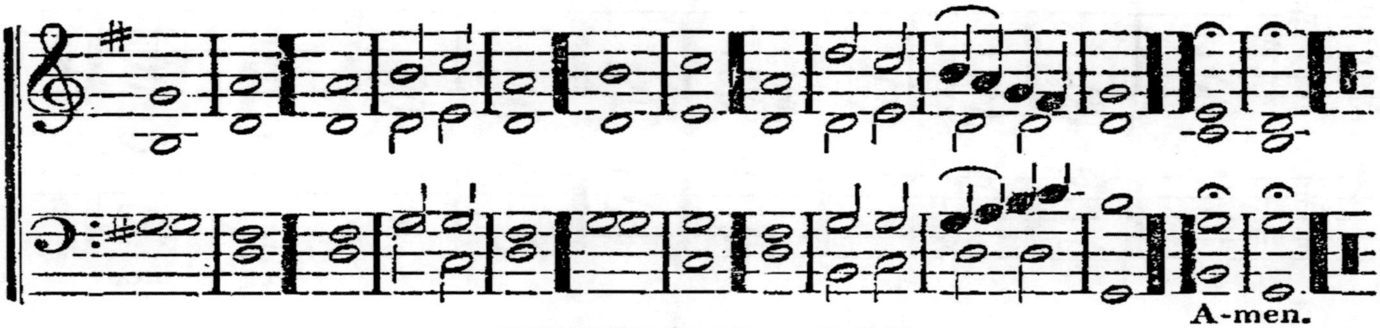

CHANT No. 142.

CHANT No. 143.

CHANT No. 144.

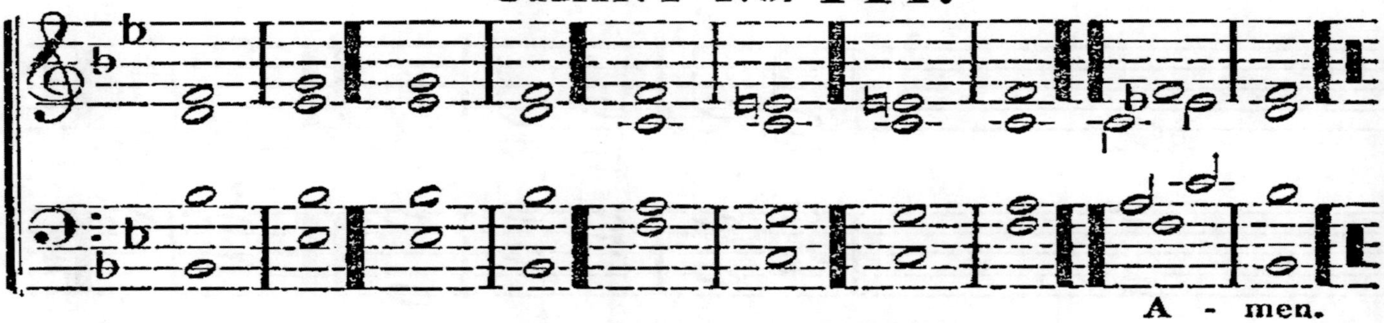

CHANT No. 145.

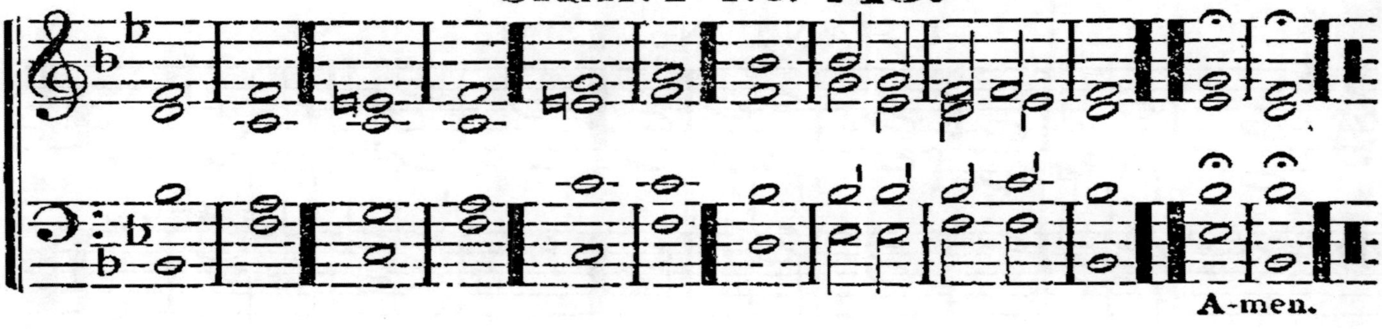

CHANT No. 146.

CHANT No. 147.

CHANT No. 148.

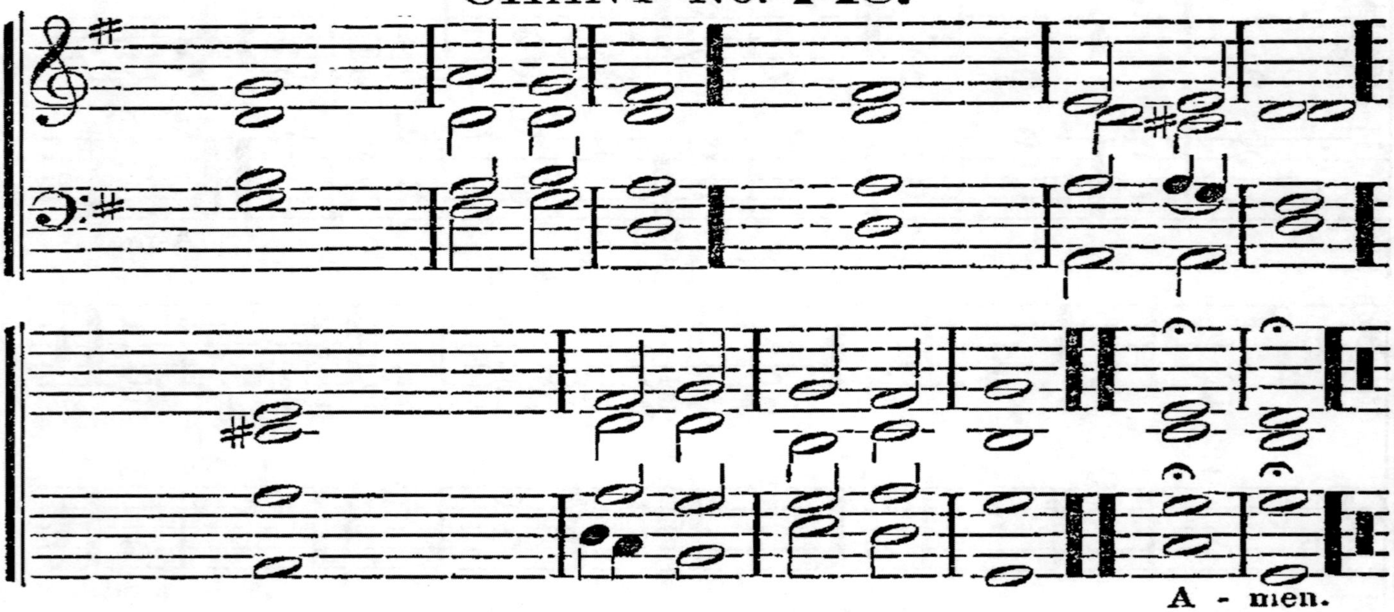

CHANT No. 149.

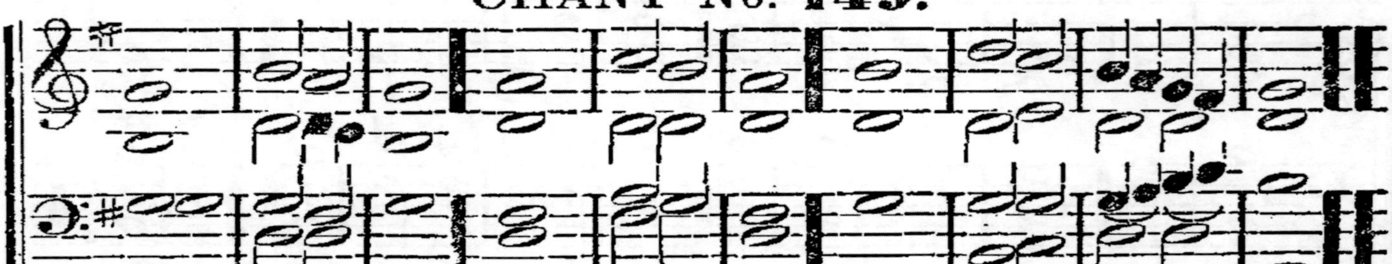

CHANT No. 150.

CHANT No. 151.

CHANT No. 152.

CHANT No. 153.

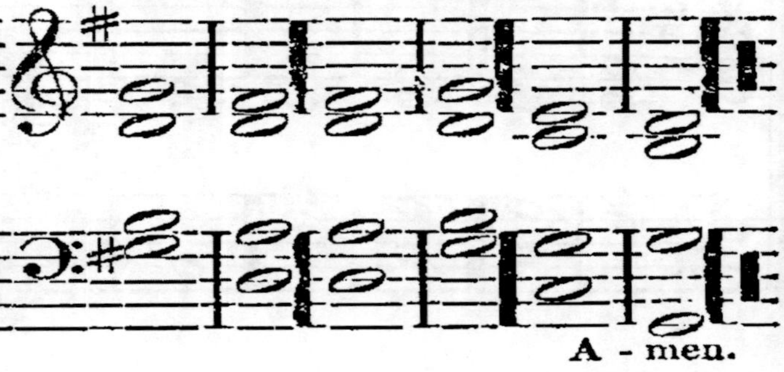

CHANT No. 154.

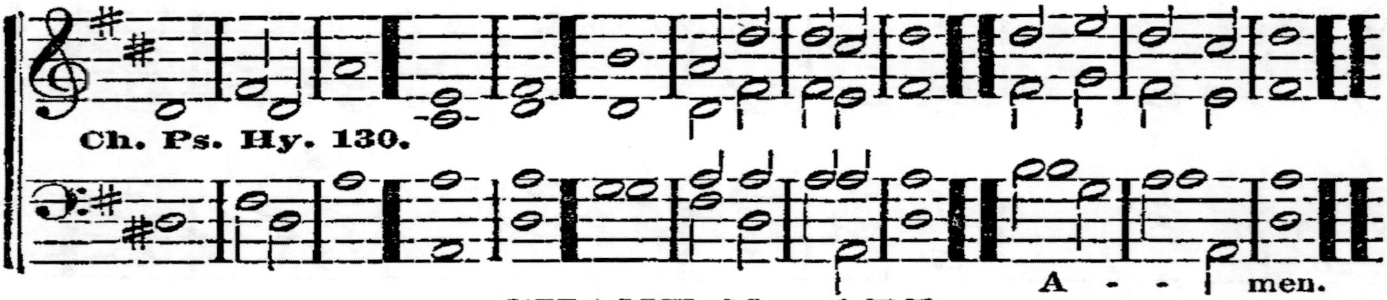

CHANT No. 155.

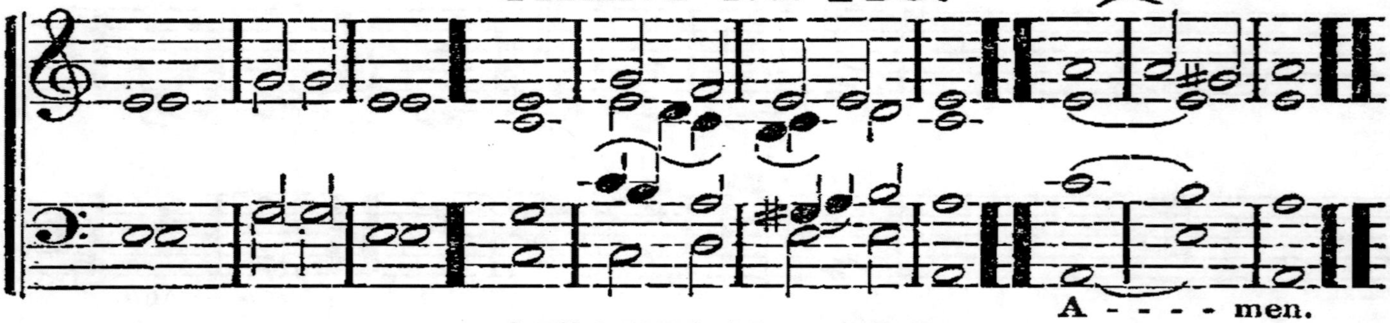

CHANT No. 156.

CHANT No. 157.

CHANT No. 158.

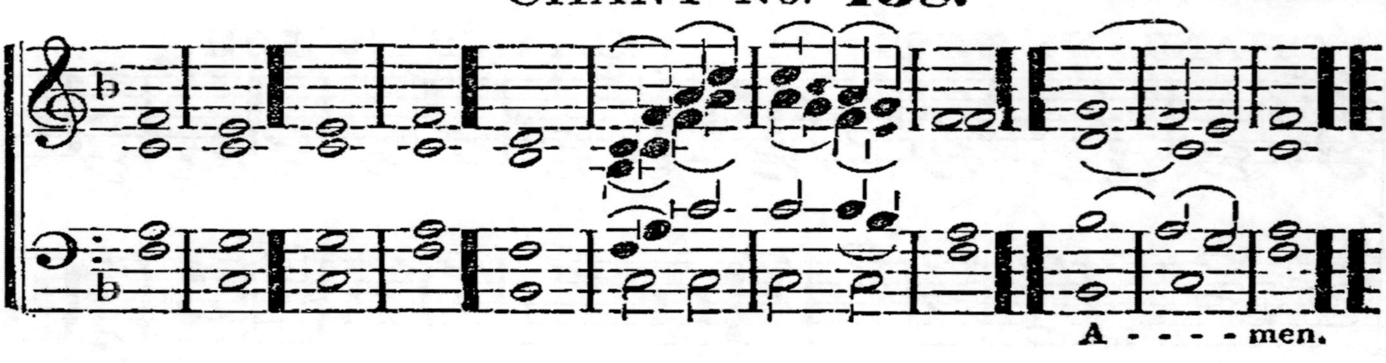

CHANT No. 159.

CHANT No. 160. (Double.)

CHANT No. 161.

CHANT No. 162.

[15]

CHANT No. 163.

CHANT No. 164.

CHANT No. 165. (Double.)

CHANT No. 166.

CHANT No. 167.

CHANT No. 168.

CHANT No. 169.

CHANT No. 170.

SELECTION. 234.

1 O Lord, open thou our | lips;
2 And our mouths shall show forth thy | praise.

3 Glory be to the Father, and to the Son, and to the Holy | Ghost;
4 { As it was in the beginning, is now, and ever shall be, world without | end.

5 Praise ye the | Lord.
6 The Lord's name be | praised.

REMARKS ON CHANTING.

There are two modes of chanting. The first or simplest form is that of the plain chant, consisting in the mere reading or reciting the words to a certain tone or given pitch, or singing to a monotone. This is heard in the daily cathedral service of the church of England, and may be illustrated by taking any convenient tone or pitch, for example, E on the third space of the staff, F clef, for male, or on the first line, G clef, for female voices, and singing to it any of the Psalms. This is probably the original mode of chanting, and is, as Latrobe supposes, the "musical pronunciation" spoken of by St. Augustin, as in use in the churches of Alexandria. Any Sabbath school may adopt this mode of chanting at once, if they are only provided with Bibles: and to give the exercise variety, interest, and impressiveness, let it be done antiphonally, or alternately by the superintendent, or some other suitable person on the one part, and the whole school, teachers and scholars on the other; the single voice singing one verse and the chorus responding in the next, and so on throughout the Psalm, adding Amen* to a common chord† at the close, if it can be conveniently done.

The other mode of chanting (Modern Chant,) to which reference has been made, adds to the chanting tone a regular cadence, and thus unites to musical recitation or reading, some of the most natural and easy progressions of melody and harmony, in connection with a few of the last words or syllables of a sentence. In addition to which it may be observed that the Modern Chant consists of two parts: 1st, a chanting note and a cadence of three notes, or parts of a measure; and 2d, a chanting note and a cadence of five notes, or parts of a measure.—Chant No. 1, is of this regular construction, and so are much the greater part of those contained in this work. In general this form of the chant is probably more satisfactory to the rhythmical sensibilities of a musical ear; but there seems to be no good reason why we should always be confined to it, and it is believed that such deviations as are found in chants Nos. 73, 75, and others, may be sometimes advantageously employed. It should be understood that the note representing the chanting tone, or pitch, is used for this purpose only: not as a rhythmical character, designating any particular length, or as bearing any proportion to the time of other notes. It is to be made longer or shorter according to the length of the verse. The words recited, or sung to this note are to be uttered about as fast as a good reader, under similar circumstances, would pronounce them; differing from good reading only with respect to pitch and inflection. The same rules, therefore, that apply to reading, in regard to enunciation, pronun-

---

*A as in Father, or Ah-men.

† If E be taken as the chanting tone, as recorded above, the chord for the Amen will be as follows.

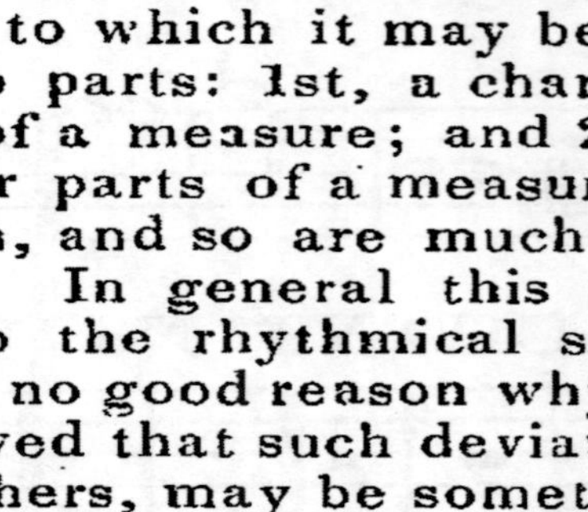

ciation, accent, emphasis, pause, and expression, are equally applicable to the reciting part of a chant. It will be obvious, therefore, that the words applied to the reciting note should not be dwelt upon, as in common singing, according to any measured time; neither should they all be of equal length; but as in good reading and speaking, so here, the important words, and especially such as express deep emotion, should occupy more time than those which are less important; the same relative proportion, in both cases, being observed.

The manner of singing the cadences must depend much upon the importance of the words, or upon the number of syllables applied to them. Although, in general, they are to be sung in time, yet strict time is not always to be observed; and although the cadence is to be performed much more like common singing, than is the chanting note, yet even here the words should receive as much of the speaking utterance and expression as is consistent with a given pitch, and a careful carriage of the voice from one tone to another.

There are two extremes in the manner of chanting which should be avoided. The first consists in allowing the voice to dwell on the sound as in common singing; or rather, perhaps, in drawling out the words, in a lingering, careless, and monotonous manner: the second, in an excessive rapidity of utterance, by which the words and sense are both in a great degree lost. A proper medium between these two extremes is desirable. Perhaps no better rule can be given than the one above mentioned, which on account of its great importance is here repeated: *Let the words be carefully delivered, to the exact pitch of the chanting note, about as fast as a good reader would utter them, and with appropriate feeling and expression.*

It may be satisfactorily proved that the Psalms were sung antiphonally or responsively to the plain chant, not only by the early Christians, but also in the earlier days of the Jewish church. This mode is equally applicable to the Modern Chant, and it is recommended as having important advantages over the more common one of singing the psalm throughout, by the whole choir or congregation. Some of these advantages are the following: It is less fatiguing; it affords greater variety; it has a tendency to keep up the attention, and to deepen impression: it is also more favorable to a simultaneous utterance of the words by a choir or congregation, inasmuch as those who respond have an example before them at the moment of singing, which they will very naturally imitate; and thus uniformity will be promoted, and the whole congregation will be kept together. Where it is practicable, it will be highly interesting to have the alternation between the clergymen and the choir or congregation. This will also have a tendency to lead all the people to regard the singing as a devotional act, which is a matter of the highest importance. But where this cannot be done, let the leader of the choir, or any other suitable person* sing the first verse, and the congregation respond in

* It is not necessary that the person who alternates with the choir should be seated with them; on the contrary, the effect will be better if he is stationed at the opposite side of the house. There can be no objection to some Miriam's taking up the single part, if there be more Miriams than Asaphs.

the second, and so on. Thus for example, in selection 2, page 6, the single voice will sing

> Give ear to my words, O Lord,
> Consider my meditation.

To which the congregation immediately respond;

> Hearken unto the voice of my cry, my King, and my Lord;
> For unto thee will I pray.

In this way, let the alternation be kept up through the whole psalm. While some of the psalms seem to be peculiarly adapted to this mode of performance, they will all admit of it with good effect.

In relation to the chanting of Metrical Psalmody, it may be remarked that it is not only suitable for such hymns* of irregular structure as are thereby rendered unfit for common tunes, but it is also equally applicable to metrical psalmody generally, much of which can be chanted with better devotional effect, than it can be sung in the ordinary way. Indeed it is safe to say, that there are but few hymns that may not be rendered more effective in chanting, at least, occasionally, than in singing to a tune or melody. The chanting of hymns after the manner proposed and illustrated in this work, is a new feature in church music, having originated, so far as is known to the editor, in the choir under his own direction; but it is one that has met the decided approbation of those who are best qualified to judge, who have had an opportunity of hearing it; and one which, it is fully believed, is destined to prevail extensively in connection with the common mode of singing. It is not difficult, and may be comparatively well done by most choirs, or even by the whole congregation. Its advantages may be gathered from what has already been said. The principal one, perhaps, is this; when a hymn is well chanted, the musical effect is rendered wholly subordinate to the sentiment. Music does indeed lend its powerful aid, but in such a modest and unostentatious way, as to be almost wholly unperceived. The sentiments, thoughts, and feelings of the hymn are thrown out in bold relief, and held up prominently as the principal thing, as in good reading. The chant, however, when well done, adds to good reading, pleasing musical tones, combinations, and progressions; and thus unites eloquence to music and poetry.

It must be observed, however, that it is only when well done that this effect is produced. A mere drawling out the sounds, in a dull and lifeless manner, is not sufficient. Nor will mere mechanical accuracy in relation to the singing of the music or the utterance of the words, although it be ever so exact, produce the proper effect. There must be indeed an ability to perform with strict accuracy, but to this must be added, in chanting as in all other singing, that life-giving, soul-moving quality, in which the vitality of all music consists, called expression; which, though no one can define, and but few impart to their performance, may be felt by all. But although it may be difficult even for a select choir, so to sing as to produce the full effect of chanting, yet it is an exercise in which, as has already been remarked, it is comparatively easy for the whole congregation to unite, and one that cannot fail to be satisfactory to those who seek for spiritual edification in their songs of praise.

---

* See p. 129.

INDEX.